SOARING ABOVE SETBACKS

SOARING ABOVE SETBACKS

The Autobiography of

JANET HARMON BRAGG

African American Aviator

as told to Marjorie M. Kriz

Smithsonian Institution Press
Washington and London

Designer: Kathleen Sims

Library of Congress Cataloging-in-Publication Data

Bragg, Janet Harmon, 1907–1993.
    Soaring above setbacks : autobiography of Janet Harmon Bragg /
as told to Marjorie M. Kriz.
        p.   cm. — (Smithsonian history of aviation series)
    Includes index.
    ISBN 1-56098-458-9 (alk. paper)
    1. Bragg, Janet Harmon, 1907–1993—Biography.   2. Afro-American
women air pilots—Biography.   I. Kriz, Marjorie M.   II. Title.
III. Series.
TL540.B693A3   1996
629.13′092—dc20
    [B]   95-41126

British Library Cataloguing-in-Publication Data is available

Manufactured in the United States of America
03 02 01 00 99 98 97 96   5 4 3 2 1

⊗ The paper used in this publication meets the minimum requirements of the American
National Standard for Information Sciences—Permanence of Paper for Printed Library
Materials Z39.48-1984.

Contents

Foreword
Johnnetta B. Cole
vii

Preface
Marjorie M. Kriz
xi

Acknowledgments
Janet Harmon Bragg
xiii

Introduction
Theodore W. Robinson
xix

1. I Become Janet
1

2. Moving North
15

3. Aviation Comes to Black Chicago
25

4. The Civilian Pilot Training Program
35

5. I Go to Tuskegee
43

6. Nursing Homes
53

7. African Students
61

8. I Go to Ethiopia
69

9. More Students and Travels
81

10. New Honors
93

11. Reflections
99

Appendix:
Friends and Colleagues
Remember Janet Harmon Bragg
107

Index
113

Foreword

In the 1930s the idea of an African American woman aviator was pre-
posterous to the majority of Americans. Black folks were said not to
be smart enough to fly, and the cockpit of an airplane was hardly a
woman's place. So what was Janet Harmon Bragg doing in 1933 as
the first woman among 27 African Americans admitted—on a segregated basis—to the Aeronautical University in Chicago? And that
was not the end of it. This led to her private pilot's license, and in
1934 Janet Harmon Bragg took off in her own 90-horsepower
biplane from an Illinois runway.

How Janet Harmon Bragg defied the prevailing assumptions about
aviation as a likely endeavor for black people, women, and most certainly those who were both, is the intriguing story of the book you
now hold in your hands. As with all biographies and autobiographies,

the success of this book must be measured not only in terms of the portrayal of a particular life, but in its explication of the times in which the central character lived. This is a successful book, as Marjorie Kriz assists Janet Harmon Bragg in telling the story of much of America as we see the life of a remarkable African American woman unfold. This autobiography is like a mirror, keenly reflecting the powerful role of racism and sexism in shaping the lives not only of women and people of color, but of the men and white Americans who lived their lives under the assumption—false as it was—that they were superior human beings.

There is something else about a successful life history. In the reading of another life, there are intersections with one's own, points where one feels touched by the people, events, experiences of the central character. This is the case even when that person lived in a different time, space, or circumstances from one's own. This clearly happened to me on so many of the pages of this very special story, for Janet Harmon Bragg's struggles against the constraints of racial and gender bias are echoed in my experiences and those of countless African American women.

But there are two very tangible ways in which my life is connected to that of Janet Harmon Bragg. The first is that her "shero," Bessie Coleman, the first African American woman aviator, was no less admired by my father, John Thomas Betsch Sr. As a young man of 21 my father witnessed Coleman's tragic death in an airplane accident in Jacksonville, Florida, the very town in which I would be born 10 years later. (See the account of this event in Doris L. Rich's book *Queen Bess: Daredevil Aviator*.)

It is through an institution called Spelman College that I am more directly connected to Janet Harmon Bragg. In her autobiography she does not speak at length about Spelman, but she speaks with respect and affection of the school—then known as Spelman Seminary—from which she graduated in nursing in 1929. While she and all the other women who attended Spelman were not encouraged to study the sciences in those days, it must have been a great joy for her to discover that today, 38 percent of Spelman students major in mathematics, the sciences, computer science, and a dual degree program in engineering.

Janet Harmon Bragg was last on Spelman's campus in 1987 to participate in a panel on Black Women in Science and Technology that was a part of the activities for my inauguration. At this symposium she gave a moving account of some of her experiences as a pioneering aviator. Janet Harmon Bragg died in 1993, on the day—April 11—exactly 112 years after Spelman was founded.

A good autobiography, a strong autobiography, must manage somehow to leave one with the sense that it is possible to "make do when don'ts want to prevail," that one can make a way out of no way. There is no shortage of this message in the autobiography of Janet Harmon Bragg.

Johnnetta B. Cole
President, Spelman College

It was through Marjorie that the FAA invited me to attend the FAA/NASA symposium at Howard University. And it was during those three days that I met some of the top people at the National Air and Space Museum. After learning more of my background, she suggested I write my autobiography. On my return to Tucson she called several times, encouraging me to write. I felt, though, that I needed her expertise as a former reporter because she knew the five W's— who, what, where, when, and why. It was Marjorie who turned over to Dr. Von Hardesty and Dominick Pisano, the "Black Wings" curators, her hefty collection of information on our Chicago achievements, provided copies of photos, gave them names and telephone numbers.

She also wrote about our achievements in articles which appeared in the FAA Great Lakes Region Intercom employee newsletter and in *FAA World,* the agency's national magazine. The latter article was reprinted for educational distribution and was listed in the "Black Wings" bibliography.

Marjorie visited me at my home in Tucson, pounding out my story on my old Sears typewriter. She was so full of life and brought a lot of sunshine into our lives. Later I visited her at her home in Evanston, where we put it all down on her computer, with her Siamese cat sitting regally on top of the machine and generally getting in the way. Marjorie was a slave driver, demanding that I come up with accurate dates and that I remember events long forgotten. This desire for accuracy didn't change as our friendship grew, because she was still demanding. She nagged me to the extent that the book got finished. My husband, Sumner, called her "our Marjorie" and was most pleased that we would be doing my autobiography. I am very grateful for her interest, her kindness, and her love.

I always will be grateful to Frances Taylor Matlock and VeNona Roberts Johnson, both retired teachers, who encouraged me to open nursing homes and gave me their moral support. My first cousin, Frances Scott Moore, also was one who was of great assistance with

Preface

The words in this book are mostly Janet Harmon Bragg's. I just rearranged them from tape recordings she made, from long letters she wrote, and from notes and dictation I took while visiting her in Tucson, where she lived year-round in a charming house with a backdrop of mountains, and in Evanston, Illinois, at my home.

I first met Janet in 1980 when I was doing research on the accomplishments of pioneer black aviators in Chicago. From the very beginning blacks had been involved in aviation, but they were few and far between and almost nothing had been documented about them in the white press or in the museums and historical societies which collect material about people and events of importance.

It was some time before I learned that Janet—believed to have been the first black woman to earn a federal commercial pilot's license (from the U.S. Department of Commerce, which handled flying licenses prior to today's Federal Aviation Administration)—also was a professional registered nurse and had successfully operated three nursing homes on Chicago's South Side. Or that she had been a surrogate mother to a large number of Ethiopian youths who had been sent by their emperor to study in the United States. Or that she was a world traveler, or that she was involved with an amazing number of other activities to aid the poor and disadvantaged—black, white, and Hispanic.

But I am not the only one to appreciate Janet's accomplishments and talents. She was much in demand as a board member for worthwhile civic projects and as a speaker on the early days in aviation. Three times I was with her at the Smithsonian Institution's National Air and Space Museum when she was honored for her early flying endeavors. And I have seen many clippings from newspapers and magazines about her achievements. But no one has told the whole Janet story, and that is what we have tried to do here, in Janet's own words. I only hope that those who will benefit most from this book, particularly young blacks and other minorities, will be among those who read it.

I long have been grateful for the opportunity to know Janet Harmon Bragg and her late husband, Sumner, and hope my efforts have been adequate in showing my appreciation.

Marjorie M. Kriz

Acknowledgments

Memories are like paintings, and each one of us has our ow[n] My gallery has so many pictures that it is filled almost to capa each one is my favorite. Are they complete? Would I like to or destroy any of them? Heck, no! Each painting is a maste[r]

I want to thank my friend Marjorie Kriz for helping me book. I first met her in 1980 at the Federal Aviation Admin (FAA) Great Lakes regional headquarters, where she was public affairs officer. Her interest in aviation history inclu black group, and it was she who put together our fir[st] exhibit, which was eventually displayed at the Smith National Air and Space Museum (NASM). She accompan and we roomed together later, at the "Black Wings" de and at other NASM events.

Preface

The words in this book are mostly Janet Harmon Bragg's. I just rearranged them from tape recordings she made, from long letters she wrote, and from notes and dictation I took while visiting her in Tucson, where she lived year-round in a charming house with a backdrop of mountains, and in Evanston, Illinois, at my home.

I first met Janet in 1980 when I was doing research on the accomplishments of pioneer black aviators in Chicago. From the very beginning blacks had been involved in aviation, but they were few and far between and almost nothing had been documented about them in the white press or in the museums and historical societies which collect material about people and events of importance.

It was some time before I learned that Janet—believed to have been the first black woman to earn a federal commercial pilot's license (from the U.S. Department of Commerce, which handled flying licenses prior to today's Federal Aviation Administration)— also was a professional registered nurse and had successfully operated three nursing homes on Chicago's South Side. Or that she had been a surrogate mother to a large number of Ethiopian youths who had been sent by their emperor to study in the United States. Or that she was a world traveler, or that she was involved with an amazing number of other activities to aid the poor and disadvantaged—black, white, and Hispanic.

But I am not the only one to appreciate Janet's accomplishments and talents. She was much in demand as a board member for worthwhile civic projects and as a speaker on the early days in aviation. Three times I was with her at the Smithsonian Institution's National Air and Space Museum when she was honored for her early flying endeavors. And I have seen many clippings from newspapers and magazines about her achievements. But no one has told the whole Janet story, and that is what we have tried to do here, in Janet's own words. I only hope that those who will benefit most from this book, particularly young blacks and other minorities, will be among those who read it.

I long have been grateful for the opportunity to know Janet Harmon Bragg and her late husband, Sumner, and hope my efforts have been adequate in showing my appreciation.

Marjorie M. Kriz

It was through Marjorie that the FAA invited me to attend the FAA/NASA symposium at Howard University. And it was during those three days that I met some of the top people at the National Air and Space Museum. After learning more of my background, she suggested I write my autobiography. On my return to Tucson she called several times, encouraging me to write. I felt, though, that I needed her expertise as a former reporter because she knew the five W's— who, what, where, when, and why. It was Marjorie who turned over to Dr. Von Hardesty and Dominick Pisano, the "Black Wings" curators, her hefty collection of information on our Chicago achievements, provided copies of photos, gave them names and telephone numbers.

She also wrote about our achievements in articles which appeared in the FAA Great Lakes Region Intercom employee newsletter and in *FAA World,* the agency's national magazine. The latter article was reprinted for educational distribution and was listed in the "Black Wings" bibliography.

Marjorie visited me at my home in Tucson, pounding out my story on my old Sears typewriter. She was so full of life and brought a lot of sunshine into our lives. Later I visited her at her home in Evanston, where we put it all down on her computer, with her Siamese cat sitting regally on top of the machine and generally getting in the way. Marjorie was a slave driver, demanding that I come up with accurate dates and that I remember events long forgotten. This desire for accuracy didn't change as our friendship grew, because she was still demanding. She nagged me to the extent that the book got finished. My husband, Sumner, called her "our Marjorie" and was most pleased that we would be doing my autobiography. I am very grateful for her interest, her kindness, and her love.

I always will be grateful to Frances Taylor Matlock and VeNona Roberts Johnson, both retired teachers, who encouraged me to open nursing homes and gave me their moral support. My first cousin, Frances Scott Moore, also was one who was of great assistance with

Acknowledgments

Memories are like paintings, and each one of us has our own gallery. My gallery has so many pictures that it is filled almost to capacity, and each one is my favorite. Are they complete? Would I like to retouch or destroy any of them? Heck, no! Each painting is a masterpiece.

I want to thank my friend Marjorie Kriz for helping me with this book. I first met her in 1980 at the Federal Aviation Administration (FAA) Great Lakes regional headquarters, where she was assistant public affairs officer. Her interest in aviation history included our black group, and it was she who put together our first photo exhibit, which was eventually displayed at the Smithsonian's National Air and Space Museum (NASM). She accompanied me, and we roomed together later, at the "Black Wings" dedication and at other NASM events.

her expertise as an interior decorator. It was a pleasure for Sumner and me to keep the homes up to standard.

I'm happy to have Tseganet M. Blumeris, my "adopted" daughter from Ethiopia, and her two children, Michael and Iris, near me in the United States. Tseganet for a time was manager of Zimbabwe tourism in the States. Michael lived with me while he was in college in Tucson. Sad to say, most of my other Ethiopian friends were slaughtered by the communist government.

The painting of our aeronautical class in Chicago is large because it includes so many people. We flew paper airplanes in the classroom just like a bunch of kindergartners. What a thrill just to touch those aircraft engines! In 1932 a visitor at one of our classes was Amelia Earhart, then not so well known as she was later. I admired her very much.

I remember how happy and helpful the people of Robbins, Illinois, were when we began to build our airport, the first black airport in the United States. They were glad to be a part of our venture. Some joined us in the hole we left on the field, which filled with enough water to be our private swimming pool.

I almost had forgotten, until another painting appeared in my mind's eye, of the summer I went barnstorming in Ohio in the early 1940s with Grover Nash.

While flying, my plane was always alive. It responded so beautifully. I could feel the rudder pedals through the soles of my feet, through the posterior part of my anatomy, when I was seated properly. I felt comfortable and at ease. I was free in spirit. I could give vent to my feelings through my maneuvers. In all, my plane and I were communicating. I would say, "Let's try a spin, two to the right," etc., or "One to the left. Are you ready?" I'd say, "Let's go." I'm sure every good pilot has done the same thing when he or she was up in the wild blue yonder.

Another of my favorite paintings is my meeting with Haile Selassie, Emperor of Ethiopia and the Lion of Judah, when he visited Chicago in 1954. How I felt is almost indescribable, as I had no idea I ever would meet a real king.

A special portrait is that of my mother, especially when I first took her up in my plane after a year of hiding from her that I was flying— and flying my own plane at that. Her fears turned to pleasure, and everything was all right. Then there is a group portrait of my parents, who taught us the meaning of love, and my brothers and sisters. We shared everything, especially love.

I always will be grateful to my husband, Sumner, who was every- thing I needed in love and happiness. He was the kindest person I've ever known. Sometimes I couldn't believe that he was real. I never felt alone after his death, because of the beautiful picture of him in my gallery. He is always there. Sometimes he would say, "May I sug- gest this. . . ." He was a true evaluator. He would comment, recom- mend, and comment again.

Sumner enjoyed beautiful and expensive clothes, and I always enjoyed shopping with him. My friends usually could tell Sumner had bought my dresses, when I was not with him. At Marshall Field's 28 shop in Chicago he would have a model show dresses to him. What it cost was not as important to him as the quality, while I think I sometimes believe in quantity, because I could buy four dresses for what he paid for one!

One of the most beautiful pictures in my gallery is the 1982 opening of the "Black Wings" exhibit at the National Air and Space Museum—one of my masterpieces. During the "Black Wings" celebration, and later at other gatherings at NASM events, I met Mrs. Noel Parrish, widow of the commander at Tuskegee during the war. She is continuing her husband's interest in encour- aging blacks to fly, and always is on hand at Tuskegee air events. I first met her late husband, in charge of cadets at Tuskegee, when I went there in 1943 to earn my commercial license, but I didn't meet her until later.

I think I've had a wonderful life: a marvelous and supportive family when I was growing up, a good academic background, a successful career helping people who were sick, a fascinating avoca- tion in aviation, a kind, gentle, and intelligent husband, marvelous friends both here and abroad, and, of late, recognition and awards from many organizations and institutions. I hope that I have encouraged others to work for careers in aviation and science— especially students unfortunately labeled as disadvantaged, for that would be the best reward.

Janet Harmon Bragg
1992

Introduction

With the life stories of many African Americans being described today in terms of overcoming almost insurmountable odds, there is a danger of our becoming inured to the superhuman strength many of these people displayed as they survived a brutal racist American white society's determination to keep them in their inferior "place." And, indeed, too many were beaten down or severely limited by the racial mores and policies of nineteenth- and twentieth-century America.

Becoming an aviator in the early 1930s wasn't easy for black people, and certainly not for black women. The legendary Bessie Coleman was forced to travel to France to learn how to fly because no flight schools in the Chicago area would accept her for the training she sought in 1920. Some ten years later, when Janet Harmon Bragg decided to pursue flight training, things had not improved much, despite the success and renown briefly achieved by "Brave Bessie." (An excellent study of the life of Bessie Coleman is Doris L. Rich's *Queen Bess: Daredevil Aviator,* published by the Smithsonian Institution Press in 1993.)

Janet Harmon Bragg's journey through life began in Griffin, Georgia, a small town south of Atlanta. She was raised by parents she remembers as loving and strict, who believed that girls could do anything boys could. This teaching was surely a prime resource to her when she decided to learn not only how to fly but also how to maintain and repair airplanes under the instruction and care of fellow aviation pioneers John Robinson and Cornelius Coffey. They recently had become the first African Americans to graduate from the airplane mechanics course offered by the Chicago-based Curtiss Wright Flying Services (later named the Aeronautical University).

Learning was valued by the Harmon family, who recognized that higher education was a way to escape the repressive molds and cracked prisms that Southern white culture used to limit black aspirations and achievements. After what was an apparently happy and academically successful high school experience, Janet attended Spelman Seminary (now College) in Atlanta and graduated with a degree in nursing.

Her early experiences as a nurse revealed to her that Southern society did not make the effort to provide adequate health and medical care for African American patients nor, for that matter, the high quality of nursing practice for which she had been trained at Spelman. She decided to leave the South, as did very many African Americans during and following World War I; all, like Janet, sought a place that would offer better opportunities and "freer air" to breathe.

What they and Janet discovered in the North was an economic environment that offered relatively better-paying jobs and a social environment that, while offering "freer air," nevertheless had its "place" for "Negroes" in segregated neighborhoods and limited access to public accommodations. With her training from Spelman and belief in herself, and despite the national economic catastrophe

of the Great Depression, Jan

nursing profession, learned ho

cessful nursing homes, and—par

the "American mother" to many

regime of Emperor Haile Selassie to

lege educations after World War II.

The reader will learn how Janet con

flung in her path because of being Afric

They will see how she used her energies for

ing the wounds she suffered from racial big

though she was the first African American wo

mercial pilot's certificate, she was denied the oppo

country as a member of the famous all-female W

Service Pilots (WASP) organization. She also was refu

to the Army Nurse Corps. She was highly qualified for

the case of her application for service with the WASP, wa

experienced white women were accepted.

She lived a creative and successful life in spite of the artifi

riers put in her path. Just before she died on April 11, 1993, in

pital in Blue Island, Illinois, a suburb bordering Chicago on

south, she told her cousin Frances Moore that they should share

room in the hospital and together write a book about their home-

town of Griffin, Georgia, and their happy life while growing up.

"We will have so much fun," she said.

Even though she had much to overcome and found little sup-

port in the wider American society, Janet Harmon Bragg tri-

umphantly affirmed her right to be the kind of achieving human

being she was. Reading about her remarkable life may help inspire

others to do the same.

Theodore W. Robinson

Series Editor, African American Pioneers of Aviation

Smithsonian History of Aviation Series

1

I Become Janet

We were a very happy family, not rich, just a little beyond poverty, but we had plenty of love and it oozed from all angles.

My hometown, Griffin, Georgia, is about 30 miles south of Atlanta. I imagine, at the time I was born, that a couple of thousand people lived there, maybe more. We used to call it the "Magic City."

My grandfather on my mother's side was of Spanish descent, though I'm sure his ancestors must have come from some part of Africa. He was a freed slave, tall, handsome, with clean features. I remember he wore his hair long. It was curly. Beautiful. His name was Oss Batts. My grandmother was a full Cherokee Indian. My mother's maiden name was Cordia Batts, and my father was Samuel Harmon. Both were native Georgians. Beyond that, I'm not interested in tracing my genealogy. I don't have time.

My grandfather Oss bought property, four or so acres of land, right after slavery time. I have the deeds showing he purchased the property in 1873. On the land he built a little house, where my mother was born. He sold it to my father when he and Mother met, and then they married. I was born in that house, as were all the children in my family. The house was destroyed, but we still have the land. I've been paying taxes on it for years and years. It was just a little outside the city limits when I was growing up, but now it's in the city. I think I would like to build decent homes on the land as a memorial to my family.

Later my grandfather bought land far from the city, and to each of his eight children he gave equal acreage. At that time I guess it was about 50 cents an acre, probably a lot of money then. He grew cotton and vegetables and had fruit trees. A rock mason, he would gather rocks from the fields and build houses with them. I remember the chimney of our house was on the outside, a huge rock chimney, and sometimes, when the sun shone on it, or just the reflection of the sun, those rocks had different colors, iridescent.

There were seven children in our family, four boys and three girls: Elza, Peter J., Samuel, Pat, Viola ("Honey"), Lillian, and me. I was the youngest. We were a very happy family, not rich, just a little beyond poverty, but we had plenty of love and it oozed from all angles. My father was a good provider. My mother worked sometimes to supplement the budget. They were able to give all of us a good education. When I think now how they managed to feed, clothe, and send seven children to school, it was a miracle. We were taught how to share, we were motivated, and we didn't forget that my father was the "head of the family." He was stern and positive, but was the kindest man ever. We had love and respect for him. He always said, "If Jack can do it, so can Jill." That meant there was no time wasted, that I was part of a family that cared, and that I could do whatever I set my sights on.

My mother was loved by the whole community. All the children in the neighborhood called her Mama Cordia. She shared with those who were less fortunate than we were. I don't remember ever hearing her say anything that wasn't complimentary, to anyone. She lived to be 86 years of age. She was precious, and every day was Mother's Day for her.

My father was a brick contractor. Most of the brick masons at that time were black; you didn't see very many whites laying bricks. I guess they thought it was slaves who used to do all this. As they just didn't want to do it, my father made a good living out of it.

Janet is a combination of my two given names: Jane Nettie. My father's mother was named Jane, and my mother's mother was Nettie, so they combined the two and called me Jane Nettie. I didn't like the name too much, though I loved my two grandmothers. It was changed for me when I was in the third grade, so I must have been about eight years old. When my teacher, Mrs. Sinclair, sent us to the blackboard, she would give us a little space to write our names. I took to writing a large "Jane Nettie" all over the board. She said, "Let's do something about this. We'll take J and A . . . N and E and T! So we have both your grandmothers' names." I thought that was smart, so that's how it started: Janet.

But I had two first cousins teaching school, one in the first grade and one in the fourth. After I had finished with third grade and went in with my fourth-grade teacher, who was my first cousin, she said, "Where did you get that name? Your name is Jane Nettie!" So through the fourth grade I had to be Jane Nettie again, but just as soon as I got out of fourth grade I went back to Janet. I could be either Jane or I could be Nettie, but I wanted to be both of them: Janet, such a pretty name.

Both of my teacher cousins were graduates of Tuskegee Institute, now Tuskegee University. One, Cora Lee, was tall and thin, the other was a little on the obese side. In those days teachers were allowed to punish students with a ruler, to spank them or strike them on the hands. My fourth-grade teacher was my obese cousin, Janie Dickens. When she ordered me to hold my hand out for punishment, I sometimes would pull it back and she'd miss. Then she'd shake all over like jelly! But both cousins were excellent teachers. A school in Griffin was later named for Cora Lee Nimmons, the slender one.

Growing up, my brother Pat and I were inseparable. We had so much to do. His name was Vanderbilt, but we called him Pat for short. I don't ever remember my brother having a fight with anybody. Never. He just didn't like violence. His sister Janet took care of him very well. I knew he wouldn't fight, but if we were coming home from school and somebody cornered him, I would walk up and that was it: "Don't touch my brother." He should have protected me. Sometimes I got the raw end of it. We were all just kids, and after two or three minutes we were all playing together as if nothing had happened. But just "don't bother my brother."

My grandfather Oss was a rather unique fellow. When he came to visit us he always drove a nice horse with a surrey with a fringe all around the top. Pat and I would go out to meet him and climb in the surrey, then he would say, "Don't put any mud in my buggy!" I probably get my saving ways from him. Every little thing I pick up I think I can use later. We used to laugh about it. When Grandfather came to visit us, he always had a pocket full of peanuts in shells. He would put his hand in his pocket, take the shells from the peanuts, then put the shells in another pocket. We thought that was funny, but it was just one of his saving ways. And he didn't want to litter. We didn't know what he did with the shells, maybe they were fertilizer for his farm.

I always liked to go out to the farm, out to his house. He had built a long walk, with white sand and cedar trees on each side, which led up to the house. It was a beautiful house, stone for the first story and frame above, with tall trees all around and a big oak in the back with a swing. Wherever he came from, he was used to beauty. I remember that sometimes he would say, "Here you are, come out to eat off your granddaddy." Then he would smile. I guess we did go out there to partake of what he had to offer, because he had watermelons, berries, plums, and all kinds of vegetables. And my grandmother made the best cookies in the country. All the good goodies were out there. But Pat would say, "I just hate to go out there. Why does he always say we go out there to eat off of him?" He didn't know Grandfather was kidding.

I thought my grandmother was so beautiful. She had long, straight black hair, and she would let my brother and me brush it. But she didn't talk much. I remember that, sometimes, we'd talk to her and her reply always was a grunt: "Um. Um." Like that. But she reared her children beautifully. My uncles and aunts were all grown when she died.

Both of my grandparents are buried in the private cemetery in the corner of our land, between two huge wild cherry trees. The limbs of the cherry trees, laden with cherries in season, were over the graves. Someone told us that it was bad luck to walk over graves, but we were not afraid. Pat and I would climb up and shake the boughs, and the cherries would fall on a sheet or quilt that Mother gave us for this special occasion. Then she would make cherry wine and let us taste it. (Sometimes we would sneak a little. After all, we were the gatherers.)

I think the real reason we were told it was bad luck to walk on graves is that they could cave in and we might fall, but it never happened to us. Also, when I was small we were told, "Don't cut your fingernails or toenails. You've got to come back and look for them when you die." Kids believed a lot of foolishness in those days.

I was a regular tomboy, climbing trees, shooting marbles. I could beat all of the boys at playing marbles. I always had a big, big bag of marbles because of my winnings. And I don't think there was a tree in our neighborhood I didn't climb. Just to look around and sit there on a limb and see the universe, and then come down. It was rather like, later, seeing the world from my airplane.

I remember I was very, very rough on my underwear. Oh yes, they were torn every day. We used to buy flour in cloth sacks, and my mother would make my panties out of the sacks. Sometimes they had letters on them. When I think about it now, they were a good commercial for flour. I could have been making money advertising this brand of flour with my panties.

Growing up, we were kind of in pairs. My father bought a Model T Ford, even though he never learned how to drive. We would go

to church in the car. Then every Sunday afternoon one pair would
have the car. One pair this Sunday, another the next, until we got
around to everybody. If my brothers had a date they could take the
car. One Sunday my father told Pat he couldn't have the car. Pat said,
"Okay," and the next day he dressed real fast and left early so he
wouldn't have to drive Father to church. When Father found Pat had
left, he asked me, "Do you know how to drive that car?"

I said, "Oh yes, sir," though I had never driven it. I got in and
turned on the switch like a veteran while my father turned the crank.
As we got it going, my mother came out and saw me. "Oh my God,
Sam, you're going to kill my child!" she cried.

Nevertheless, I drove him to church. I didn't know how to back
up, but we got home safe and sound. There was only one dangerous
part anyway: when we came down the little driveway there was a
sharp turn to avoid a ditch across the road. But I made it all right. I
could reach the pedals well enough, but needed a pillow so I could
see out the windshield.

Pat was already at church when we arrived. He whispered, "How
did you get here?" I said, "I drove the car." He said, "You don't
know how to drive the car." I said, "I did drive it. I do know."
When we returned home, my mother said to my father, "Don't you
ever do that again." I guess I must have been about 12 or so. I still
like to drive.

My mother was an excellent cook. She was the kind who didn't
have to measure anything. A pinch of this and a pinch of that, put it
all together, and it would come out just right. Her biscuits were
heavenly. I remember, when I was 14 or 15, going with her to
county fairs where she made her famous biscuits. One time a white
woman asked Mother for her biscuit recipe. Another woman, who
was ahead of her at the booth, said, "Oh, they don't use recipes." Of
course, I was helping my mother and said, "Oh yes, she has a recipe."
So when we got home that night I said, "Mother, let's get these
things together, so make some biscuits." When she put in a pinch of
something I had a spoon there to measure, and that's how I got the

recipe. The next day at the fair I told the women my mother had the recipe, but I didn't give it to them. I just wanted them to know my mother *had* a recipe.

Mother made a great sweet potato pone. I should have stayed with her to learn how to make it. She grated the sweet potatoes, added spices, honey, and nuts, and baked it like a pie: a marvelous dessert. Those old recipes are things nobody knows today. I regret I didn't get many of her beautiful recipes. It makes me unhappy when I realize now what a treasure they would be. Sometimes you don't know these things until it's too late.

Mother often told us imaginative stories. Maybe she made up some of them. Like Brother Rabbit in the briar patch: Brother Rabbit did something bad, or stole something. I don't remember now exactly what it was. Somebody caught him and said, "I'm going to kill you," and the rabbit said, "Oh, please do. I'm not fit to live with." "I'm going to kill you. I'm going to pull your ear off," and the rabbit replied, "Oh, please pull my ear off, because I don't need any ears. I don't listen." He was going to have his nose cut off, and his eyes out. Finally, "I'm going to throw you in the briar patch," and the rabbit said, "Please don't throw me in the briar patch, because it will scratch me all over." Then he was thrown in the briar patch, and he ran off, laughing, "Ha, ha! This is where I was born and reared."

There was a moral there, the way she told it, because we had to listen. If your ears are pulled off you can't listen, and if your nose is cut off you can't smell. There were many stories she told with a good moral; some she invented and some she read. I remember many of them today.

My older sister, Viola, was more strict with me than my mother. She was "mother" when my mother was away. Even before she went to Tuskegee Institute, where she majored in home economics, she was doing most of the housekeeping, making my clothes, and mending those of my brothers. Later she practiced on us what she learned at college. When it was time for her to go away to school, packing her bags and all, I began crying a couple of weeks beforehand. She was a beautiful person, very petite, and I loved her. Anything she said, that was it. At that time we called her "Honey," a pet name.

We had a garden full of all kinds of vegetables and some fruit trees. Peaches—you know, Georgia is the peach state—lovely peaches, apples, cherries. At one time my father opened a little grocery store next to the house. He said we ate up all the profits, which we did. Later he closed the store and gave it to a woman from Tupelo, Mississippi, Janie Beeks, who had married one of his best friends. She wanted to teach school and turned it into a classroom, a little private school. It turned out to be very good. I don't remember how long she taught there.

When I was a child, oh, four or five years old, I sometimes played alone on the lawn. I would lie on the grass and look up in the sky and when there were big cumulus clouds I always heard a song in my mind: "There's Not a Friend Like the Lonely Jesus." Only I thought it was the "long-legged Jesus" and I would imagine Him walking over those clouds with his long legs, and it was like snow or slush over the clouds. I thought I would like to go up there and see what it was like. Years later, when I was taking flight lessons, I thought about it again, but I was always told to avoid the clouds because you didn't know what was inside them. It wasn't so slushy after all.

We were an ecumenical family. Everybody went to a different church. My father said, "As long as we serve the Lord." My mother and one sister were Baptists, another sister was a Methodist. My father, Pat, and I were Episcopalians. My other two brothers visited any church where their girlfriends were members, but they went to church.

Father didn't like the less formal churches because the members shouted. I liked the music at these churches because it was kind of swingy. We were supposed to be really proper, going to church. In the Baptist church they did shout, and some old sister sitting next to you would feel the spirit, throw her arms, and knock you about like a tumbleweed. Then we would start relaxing, and the next church would be maybe the Methodist, which was not quite as shouty. The Episcopal church was the quietest.

After the Episcopal church was organized in my mother's kitchen, then the members built the church itself. My father laid the foundation, and the diocese sent a priest, Father John Brooks. He came from the West Indies to take charge of the church, and lived in our house. My father asked some of the members, who had helped build the church, and their friends to come for a little meeting with the priest, a charming man, handsome, with a delightful accent. My mother had prepared a lovely supper. She suggested we open with a prayer, but Father Brooks couldn't find his prayer book. Mother, an old Baptist lady, got up and said one of those fine prayers which go straight up to heaven.

I didn't know whether I wanted to be part of the Episcopal church, because it was so staid, but once the church was finished, St. Stephens, we built a school and I transferred from the public school to St. Stephens Episcopal School. It was a private school, with good, strict teachers.

While I was growing up, we had only one high school for blacks in Griffin. When it was my time to go, my father decided to send me down to Fort Valley, Georgia, to an Episcopal boarding school. It was not too far away, but we had to go by train. It was a good school, where I did exceptionally well in math, physics, and science, which served me well throughout my adult life, both as a registered nurse and in my avocation, flying. The teachers were strict, but caring and patient, which meant we had to succeed. I realized that with a good foundation I could build anything on it.

The campus was nice, with five or six buildings: a chapel and the president's home, a building for classrooms, and also a girls' and a boys' dormitory. I enjoyed it very much. One of my teachers, a Canadian, was fond of me and liked my athletic ability. "I can give Janet Harmon a football and she can carry it across the field," he said. I played basketball and volleyball and all the sports for girls. I was a very good tennis player, too.

Pat, who had gone to high school in Griffin, came to see me almost every month. "Janet, your brother is here," someone would call up to the third floor where my room was, and I would tear down the steps, not like a lady, and hug him, knocking his packages all over the ground. He would always have a big box of food and clothing from my parents.

In history class one of my classmates, who sat behind me, never studied. I don't know whether he was just one of those smart fellows. When the teacher called on him to recite the assignment, he would get up and ad lib. When we had to turn in our papers so she could correct them, he never had a paper. "Janet, give me your paper," he would say, and I would say, "I'm not going to give you my paper." "You take it up there and let her see it and bring it back to me. Don't put your name on it." I did just what he told me to do; guess I was kind of sweet on him.

One girl, whom I met again years later, when Lena Horne became so popular, said, "You must remember Lena Horne. I think she was there at Fort Valley when you were." But I didn't remember her.

In school we had a "Blue Vein Society," and I was president. When the president and principal, Professor Harold Hunt, heard about this Blue Vein Society he ordered us to his office. When we arrived at his book-filled room, he asked, "Who is the leader of this group?" Everyone pointed to me. There were different colors in this Blue Vein Society—Lillian Greene, a very pretty girl, was really light-skinned, and Mattie Glasco was olive-colored. Professor Hunt put an end to it quickly. He demanded, "Do you know what it means?" I said, "No, but we've all got blue veins." And he said, "I can't see your veins at all." Very curtly, I replied, "But they *are* blue." We didn't know what "blue vein" meant, but we liked the sound of it.

High school at Fort Valley was a turning point in my life. The teachers, all very competent, sent us to charm classes, something I needed very badly. They taught us how to sit and stand and be quiet. How to get ourselves all together. It was a big improvement, for when I finished my first year and returned home for the summer, everybody said, "What's wrong with Janet? She's changed. She thinks she's something because she went away to school." But it wasn't that, it was just the training I was getting, and that I needed after being such a tomboy. Besides, I was growing up. My parents knew that sending their child to a boarding school was the right thing to do.

During summer vacation, after church every Sunday we went to one of our friends' houses for dinner, or they came to our house. It was very nice. All my friends were growing up. My friend Margaret Stokes's family had a funeral home. Margaret and I wanted to go to a dance one night, out in the country someplace. We had permission to go, but we had no way to get there. My brother Pat took his girl in our car, and Margaret's brother took their car with his girl.

Margaret said, "Daddy, you know one thing? Sam took the car. He could've taken us. Why didn't he?"

"Well, no young man on a date wants his sister along," he replied.

"We don't have a way to get out there," she said. "Then take the hearse!" Mr. Stokes said. Well, we did. Margaret drove. Everyone who saw the big black hearse thought somebody had died. It was just fun for us. It always was really clean fun.

There was one older fellow who always had a big car, Biddy Phillips. He owned a Hudson Super 6, a black, four-door monster. "This is my Hudson Super 6," he'd say, and take a gang of us out in the country for a drive. Once, we got way out in the country some-where, maybe six miles from home. "Oh, I'm out of gas," Biddy said. We all started looking at each other. "I'm out of gas, and I don't know what we're going to do." Margaret, Cora Nelms, and I had to be home before dark, and the sun was just about its own width from the horizon. Oh Lord, don't let the sun go down! We ran all the way home. Though we were socializing with others our own age, we still had to be home when our parents wanted us to be.

Biddy was a very comical person. One time he was caught speed-ing. The police arrested him and he had to go to court. When the arresting officer told the judge Biddy had been speeding, Biddy said, "Oh no, judge. He's wrong. He said I was doing 45 miles an hour. Judge, I was doing 55 miles an hour, and I wanted to see how many miles I could get out of that car because that is my Hudson Super 6." Well, the judge cracked up and ruled, "Case dismissed. Don't you do that again."

In Griffin we had our own movie theaters. The first one was down Sleighton Alley, where we didn't have to go up in what we called the "buzzards' roost" (the segregated section) to see pictures. Jimmy Gray, a photographer, was in charge of the theater. We saw all the same pictures shown on the main street. Later, a Mr. Connolly built a beautiful large theater for blacks on one of our main streets. We saw all the great pictures of the day there. We had a pianist to accompany the silent films and great popcorn and candy in a very nice lobby.

After I graduated from Fort Valley in 1925, my parents sent me to Spelman Seminary (later College) in Atlanta, rather than to Tuskegee Institute, which my sisters had attended. Like them, I was a home economics major, but after the first year I switched to nursing. I think I was influenced by an older cousin, Pauline Dickens Hall, a nurse who had graduated from Tuskegee. She looked so gorgeous in her heavily starched white uniform and seemed to know everything. She was tall and stately, and when she walked the starch was so stiff she seemed to rattle. She gave talks on health to students in the public schools, and I was very much impressed with her knowledge.

My cousin Frances Scott (later Moore) and I spent the summer with Pauline, then a public health nurse in Macon, Georgia. We were "sweet" on the same little fellow. Frances said to me, "Don't let T. C. kiss you, because Hon [Pauline] is a nurse and she can tell. She knows everything." I became doubly impressed. I thought Pauline was a clairvoyant, but I found out differently after I became a nurse.

Spelman's MacVicar Hospital was small but well equipped, and every division was outstanding. The staff doctors were good, and the head nurses and teachers were dedicated white professionals. There was no playing around for nursing students. We had to work, knowing there was a six-month probationary period. If we didn't come up to par we were eliminated. In my class of twelve, only two of us were left after six months: my roommate, Frances Lucille Davis from Mobile, Alabama, and me. We roomed together for our last three years.

MacVicar had no interns, so the nursing students had to assume their duties, assisting in operations. That was fascinating. We really knew our _Gray's Anatomy,_ we knew _Materia Medica._ We took care of all postoperative cases, changing dressings, putting in drainage. We were trained in many medical techniques that were important to the welfare of the patients.

Our senior year was a "wrangler"—we were on call at all times and in any part of the hospital. We had to make the right decisions about who to call, as almost all of the emergencies happened at night. All of the doctors, the head nurses, and the hospital superintendent had to rely upon the black student nurses for most of the everyday (and every-night) work. Much of the time we could and would take care of an emergency ourselves, write it up, go back to bed, and get up at 6 A.M. ready to report for 7 A.M. duty.

I had excellent, super training at Spelman. Today, if I were to go to Spelman, I think I would be a part of the National Aeronautics and Space Administration's program there to encourage black women to enter aerospace and science fields. During my day, though, there was no space program, and women majored in home economics, nursing, music, and literature. Women were not encouraged to study the sciences.

I therefore left Spelman well trained for a career in nursing. But I was relatively unprepared for the working world's hardships and injustices.

2

Moving North

It didn't take me long to realize that de facto segregation existed in the North as much as it did in the South—the only difference was that you didn't have to ride in the back of the bus.

After graduation from Spelman and MacVicar Hospital, I worked for a month in Griffin. All of our neighbors were so proud of me. It was a white hospital; I worked in the small segregated area in the basement, where blacks were given inferior care. While I was there, one of our favorite neighbors gave birth to a son. Afterward, she began hemorrhaging and no one made any attempt to do anything for her. I could do nothing to help, because everything had to be done under a doctor's orders. She died from loss of blood and other complications which, I'm sure, would have been no problem if attended to immediately.

Another one of my childhood friends, Ed Henderson, came in for a tonsillectomy. He said he wouldn't go to the hospital unless I stayed with him until after his tonsils were removed. Shortly after the surgery I noticed he was hemorrhaging, so I reported it to the head nurse on the ward.

"Oh, he'll be all right," she replied. I didn't think so and put an ice collar around his neck and asked the head nurse to report Ed's condition to his doctor. She refused, so I went outside the hospital and made the call myself.

The doctor came over immediately and noted the ice collar. "This is good," he said. The head nurse said, "I did it," but I corrected her. "Oh no, you didn't. I did. It's just routine." The doctor put in some sutures, and Ed went home that same night, saying he wasn't going to stay any longer.

After these two episodes in the hospital, I didn't go back to work. I knew I could not take the way they treated—or didn't treat—the black patients after knowing how we would have done something at MacVicar.

Shortly after I had quit working at the Griffin hospital, my sister Viola, who had taught school in Detroit after graduation from Tuskegee, came home to Griffin for a visit. I had not seen her for eight years. She invited me to visit her and her husband, Fred Davis, at their new home in Rockford, Illinois, and look for work there. I wanted to go, but I didn't want to leave my parents. The next summer, however—this was in 1930—I took the train to Rockford to stay with Viola and Fred. I was ready for a new life.

At that time, there weren't too many blacks living in Rockford. Viola's husband, Fred, and many of their friends were Tuskegee Institute graduates. One of her best friends was Viola Smith, whose husband, Roland, had been a classmate of Fred's at Tuskegee. Just to keep the two Violas straight, Fred started calling my sister "Sophia," and for more than twenty-five years she was Sophia Davis to all of her friends in Rockford.

When I wasn't hunting (unsuccessfully) for a job, I helped my sister with the housework. She and Fred were very kind to me, introducing me to all of their friends and treating me as one of their family, albeit still like a little sister. She and Viola Smith took me to dances and concerts, as Fred didn't like to go. I enjoyed the community even though I couldn't find work.

After nearly a year, I was getting pretty discouraged, but then I met Mrs. Willie Carey, a registered nurse from Chicago visiting her family in Rockford. She and her sister had graduated from the Provident Hospital School of Nursing. Provident was one of the country's best-known black hospitals, a pioneer in a number of medical procedures. Mrs. Carey persuaded me to stay with her in Chicago and look for work there.*

Mrs. Carey and her sister, Bertha DePriest, made me most welcome. Bertha, whom we called "Bun," introduced me to many of her friends. Willie, a public health nurse, was a churchgoer. Every morning when she awoke she would sing the 27th Psalm: "The Lord is my light and my salvation, whom shall I fear? The Lord is the stronghold of my life, of whom shall I be afraid?" To this day I, too, sing the 27th Psalm every morning. It gives me strength to cope with any problems which may arise.

I had taken a big step leaving the South, and now I had left my sister in Rockford and moved to Mrs. Carey's three-flat building on Chicago's South Side, called Bronzeville in those days. It didn't take me long to realize that de facto segregation existed in the North as much as it did in the South—the only difference was that you didn't have to ride in the back of the bus. Getting a job, regardless of a good education, was almost impossible. Many of our professional men—lawyers, physicians, dentists, teachers—had to work nights in the post office to earn a decent living. Many were Pullman porters or cooks on the railroads. To "run on the road" or work at the post office enabled many blacks to earn funds for higher education and to set themselves up in offices to pursue their chosen professions.

---

*African American migration from the South to the North intensified during the 1920s and 1930s, having begun in a sizable way during World War I. The impact on Chicago and other Northern cities was the creation of large concentrations of black citizens deliberately segregated on the basis of race. The principal force driving the migration was the desire to escape Southern racism and violence. Chicago, like other Northern cities, offered at least a glimmer of possibility for better-paying jobs and improved living conditions.—*Ed.*

I was determined to find my destiny, a position as a nurse, but first I had to take the state licensing exam to practice professional nursing in Illinois. The tests were given alternately in Chicago and Springfield, the capital, and as I didn't want to wait for the next Chicago session I went to Springfield, which led to my first experiences with racial bias in the North.

On the Greyhound bus going south from Chicago's Loop I met two other black nurses who were to take the test. We left very early so that we could make the trip, take the five-hour test, and get back home the same day. There was an empty seat next to a white woman who was leaning out of the window talking to friends. I asked if anyone were sitting in the vacant seat, and she said, "No," but to her friends on the platform she remarked, "This is what I don't like about your state. You have to sit next to people you don't want to." I suggested that one of us could move, but she declined. The Chicago area was less segregated, at least on buses, than Springfield.

Luckily, we had no more difficulties on the bus and arrived on time for the test. On our lunch break, however, when my two new friends from the bus and I walked over to the nearest drugstore for a hamburger, we found that Springfield, once the home of Abraham Lincoln, was still segregated. We were refused service at the lunch counter, but were told we could buy our food if we ate elsewhere. So, as we had no time to argue, we ate our hamburgers in the park and returned to the test room. The test did not prove too difficult; I passed with high marks and became a professional registered nurse in Illinois.

In Chicago only three hospitals—Provident, Wilson, and Cook County—hired black nurses, so I made applications at all of them. None had any positions available, so I did private-duty nursing for more than a year—and hated it. Two or four hours off was possible, but only if you could get someone to relieve you. During the Depression, few people had enough money to employ a registered nurse, even though the going wage was only $7 for twenty-four hours of duty. Other private-duty nurses I talked to told me to ask this question before I put on my uniform: "Who will be responsible for my bill?" and to say "I want my pay every day." I had to learn the hard way, but it paid off. I usually got at least some of my money, although part of the time I was short-changed badly.

On one case I took care of one of Chicago's big-time gamblers, "Big Jim." He and his wife lived in the 3300 block of South Rhodes Avenue in a huge apartment, about seven or eight rooms, very lavishly furnished. They had many theatrical friends. Bill "Bojangles" Robinson, the great dancer, was a frequent visitor. I was surprised to find that Bojangles could neither read nor write. He would bring all of his letters for Big Jim's wife to read, but he would remember, verbatim, what was read to him. It made me wonder why people who could not read or write would make no effort to learn. That would not have been possible in my family. We all wanted to learn.

I became a member of the Chicago Graduate Nurses Association, and I still hold membership. There were many women—black and white—from different schools of nursing. The Chicago chapter was a member of a national body; all of us worked hard—fight, fight, fight—to keep all graduate professional nurses walking in dignity, though at times we had to take other jobs.

One member, a Mrs. Garcia, was working at a lampshade factory. She told me the work wasn't hard and that I should try it. I did. When I went with her to the factory, she told me to tell the boss I'd had six months' experience. Sure enough, the woman asked how much experience I had, and I told her six months. But she knew I was lying and would not let me sit with Mrs. Garcia, who was going to instruct me. Instead, she gave me one of the hardest shades to make, a "drum" lining.

I worked on that darn shade all day and earned thirty-five cents. I was too embarrassed to go back the next day, even though the woman told Mrs. Garcia she wanted me to return. The factory, on Indiana Avenue, was ill-lighted and dirty, paint was peeling off the walls. It was cold, and the woman in charge was really a nasty, hard-boiled person.

One day about six of us, all graduate nurses, went looking for jobs. Someone had told us we could get work at one of the big downtown hotels, working at night at the Palmer House, the Stevens—then the world's largest hotel—and several others. We felt that if we were really presentable it would be easier to get one of these jobs, so we all got dressed up. I wore my best navy blue suit, with a white blouse, blue shoes, silk hose, a cock hat, and even gloves.

There we were, standing in line, so erect and looking too intelligent, waiting to be picked to fill a vacancy as a hotel maid. Several other women were also in line, none looking too tidy; one even had a "dip" of snuff in her lip. Well, they were selected and we weren't. The housekeeper told us to try again.

We did make another attempt, but this time we didn't dress up and, yes, we got the jobs and earned a new title: "hotel maid." I became a "bath maid." I thought I would be helping with giving baths to rich ladies for, after all, as a nurse I was well acquainted with giving baths. But no, I had to clean all the bathrooms. I cleaned so many bathrooms at the Palmer House I dreamed about them in my sleep.

I was too tired to get up to go to work the next day, which turned out to be a good thing because I received a telephone call to come to the Wilson Hospital at 30th Street and Vernon Avenue to be interviewed for the night supervisor job for which I had applied. The salary wasn't too much, but anything was better than making lampshades or scrubbing bathrooms. Nursing was my profession, something for which I had trained, and I loved it.

As the night supervisor, I was in charge of the emergency room as well as the rest of the small hospital. The emergency room always was a fascinating part of the hospital, as I never knew what was coming next. I just had to be prepared for anything. From Friday night through Sunday morning, and on holidays, there were accidents of all descriptions. Shootings, cuttings, stabbings, even births—you name it.

I remember one night when the police brought in an emergency case, a man who had been cut from the nape of his neck to his buttocks. It was a night when Joe Louis, the Brown Bomber, was fighting at the Chicago Stadium, and only one intern was on duty. I was in charge of the operating room when the policeman brought the man in and put him on the table.

It was routine to swab a wound with an antiseptic—iodine was preferred because it deadened the nerves to such an extent that it was bearable when you had to use sutures to close the wound. As I cleaned the man's gaping wound, swabbing him from head to buttocks with iodine, he screamed to high heaven, praying and cussing all at the same time. The intern started to suture the wound, but took one stitch and fainted, passed out completely. Here I had a doctor on the floor and a man bleeding to death on the table. I had two alternatives: I could try to revive the doctor, or I could suture the patient myself. I took fifty-six stitches in the patient, praying and cussing along with him. He was put to bed and somehow survived.

The intern made me promise not to tell anyone about the episode, and to this day I have never divulged his name. That night I thanked God for Spelman's MacVicar Hospital and for my super training there. That night I also recalled my first day in the operating room at Spelman, when I was the scrub nurse. A fellow's arm was amputated. I held the basin to receive it, and when the arm hit the basin I hit the floor. Knowing how I had felt then, I knew how hurt and embarrassed Dr. X was. My classmates never talked to anyone about my incident with the arm, and I never mentioned Dr. X's collapse.

Right behind Wilson Hospital, at 38th Street and Rhodes Avenue, was the Chicago Medical School, which I attended for the two years I worked at Wilson. I studied laboratory procedures and radiology, which resulted in the offer of a laboratory job in Andrew Hospital at Tuskegee Institute. By then I was engaged to marry Evans Waterford, however, so I gave up the idea of returning to the South to work and got married instead. Evans Waterford was an educated man, from LeMoyne-Owen College in Memphis, but, like many talented black men of the time, was unable to obtain a position commensurate with his background and had to do odd jobs. We met at Wilson Hospital, where he had come to visit a relative. The marriage lasted only two years, and we were divorced due to incompatibility.

After my divorce it became obvious that I would have to get a better job. My father had died at 75 after a long illness, and my mother and two nieces, Cordia Beeks and Evelyn Harmon, who had come to Chicago to stay with me, needed my support.

So I took a position doing triple duty as a nurse working for three doctors—a general practitioner; an eye, ear, nose, and throat specialist; and a dentist—all in the same office suite. Those years were rewarding, especially what I learned from the late Dr. Claudius Forney, the ENT man, for whom I worked for ten years, adding considerably to my knowledge. I studied at night at Loyola University on Chicago's North Side, earning a certificate in a graduate course in public health administration. I also took graduate work in pediatric nursing at the Cook County Hospital School of Nursing.

To take advantage of my graduate training, I decided to look for a city public health job. For the first time I had to learn how the great political machine governed who would or would not get to work in Chicago. It was Edward ("Mike") Sneed, for many years a powerhouse as a Cook County commissioner, and the only black member on the board which governed Cook County Hospital, whose favor had to be curried for a nursing job at a welfare maternity clinic. I knew that much, but not about the all-important political pyramid which had to be scaled before reaching Sneed.

Instead of starting with my Democratic precinct captain—I didn't even know his name, let alone where he could be found—I went straight to the top and presented myself at Sneed's South Side political office at 47th Street and South Parkway (now Martin Luther King Jr. Drive).

"Who sent you?" the receptionist asked. I said no one had sent me, that I'd come about a job. "Well, who is your precinct captain?" I

didn't know that either. "I just want to see Mr. Sneed," I said. "I need a job and this is the place to come."

I guess Commissioner Sneed could hear both of our voices rising. He came on the intercom and told the receptionist to let me in. Tall and thin and handsome, and looking not at all like the powerful politician he was, Sneed laughed at my ignorance, then told me to see Daisy Sampson, who operated a sort of clearinghouse for nurses hired for the program.

I turned up early the next morning at Daisy's office at 43rd and State streets to find a crowd already waiting, but no Daisy. My wait wasn't too long for this chunky martinet, a graduate nurse, but what happened next really astounded me. Everyone stood up and saluted her, just like soldiers. Yes, I mean saluted, like people in the military saluting a superior officer. As I didn't know about the system, let alone what to think of the saluting business, I remained seated. Daisy came over to me and asked who I was and why I didn't stand up. I told her I needed a job and was qualified as a nurse. I just couldn't believe blacks would demand this sort of obeisance from other blacks, and I finally left and went back to Sneed's office.

Amazingly, Sneed didn't know about Daisy's method of operating, or said he didn't. Anyway, he said he would see that those seeking jobs in the future would not have to salute her anymore. Eventually, because of my background and training, I was offered a job as a social worker at a city clinic. This hardly pleased me as, after all, I felt my profession was nursing. Another woman offered to switch with me so I could go back to nursing, but by then I was thoroughly disillusioned and refused, deciding instead to look elsewhere.

Through the Chicago Graduate Nurses Association, of which I eventually became president, I had met and become good friends with Ann Giddings, a graduate of the Meharry Medical College School of Nursing. She was working at the Metropolitan Burial Insurance Association (now the Chicago Metropolitan Assurance Company) and offered to introduce me to the manager. I was hired, and so for the next ten years I worked as a health inspector a

Metropolitan, adding again to my knowledge of nursing and of people in general. I was really more of a detective than a nurse, though being a nurse was required, much as the first airline stewardesses had to be nurses. The company would learn that insurance had been written for a person the agent thought was healthy, when actually that person was a "ringer" for someone already sick and in a hospital. My job was to visit the insured, after the agent wrote a policy, determine the actual health of the insured, and reject those who didn't pass inspection. Each case required obtaining a social history of the insured and comparing the signature of the person I visited with that the agent had procured. The staff of six nurses was like family.

I was beginning to feel settled at last in my professional life. Meanwhile, I was already experiencing some other adventures—in the air.

3

Aviation Comes to Black Chicago

Finally, with thirty-five solo hours, I was ready to take
the test for a private pilot's license. The federal examiner,
a very nice white man, said, "It doesn't matter what
color you are, just that you know what you are doing."
With the good instruction I had received, I did.

I suppose that, in the back of my mind, I had been interested in flying since my childhood reveries of a long-legged Jesus walking on
the clouds. But I just wasn't aware of it, although I had watched
planes land at the fairgrounds across from our home in Griffin.
Thanks to some financial success through steady employment, almost
from the beginning of my arrival in Chicago, I became involved in
aviation, an avocation which I pursue to this day, and which has
brought me national honors and awards as well as personal satisfac-
tion. My friends in aviation also led me into other pursuits, which
resulted in extensive travels in Africa and Europe and a friendship
with Ethiopian Emperor Haile Selassie and his family.

These days we think of the 1920s and '30s as the golden years of
aviation, no less so for blacks, despite the rampant discrimination and

bias of those times. In a way we were lucky to have discovered our love of aviation during this time of national excitement. Our own eagerness was part of America's love affair with the airplane. But in the 1920s and '30s, and even later, aviation was not considered to be a suitable pursuit for blacks, who were deemed unable, both mentally and physically, to fly safely. Although a black man, Eugene Bullard, flew with the French Flying Service in World War I, his achievements are mostly overlooked. But for a black woman to fly—well, that just wasn't done, except for the extraordinary Bessie Coleman, who had to go to France to receive flight training. And Bessie had died in 1926.

One day in Chicago I saw a billboard with a bird sitting on the rim of a nest, nurturing her young fledglings into the flying world. It read, "Birds Learn to Fly. Why Can't You?" That did it. It was so beautiful. I can see it now. As children, my brother Pat and I had watched birds fly, flaring their wing and tail feathers on alighting on a branch or on the ground, where we would feed them crumbs. We noticed the way they always seemed to come in against the wind, just as with an airplane. The sign and my recollections motivated me to start making inquiries as to where I could go to learn to fly.

One fall evening I read in the *Chicago Defender,* one of the nation's most prestigious black newspapers, about aviation ground-school classes to be held for blacks at the Aeronautical University, formerly a Curtiss Wright school. My schooling had prepared me for ground school, as I had done very well in math, physics, and sciences, both in high school and college. Classes were to be held two evenings a week and would not interfere with my nursing sleuth work at Metropolitan.

I drove to the first class at 14th Street and Michigan Avenue in my dark blue Ford coupe (required in my work), and with notebook in hand walked excitedly into the classroom and sat down in one of those chairs which has an arm to write on. None of it was what I expected; the first session—and many to follow—concerned meteorology, a knowledge of which is still required for those working toward a private pilot's license.

The instructors were Cornelius Coffey and John Robinson, two black men about as different as they could be, both in looks and personality. Coffey was small and thin, very serious about safety in flying, strict, professional, and fair to everyone, and everyone loved him. Robinson was tall and muscular, ebullient, adventurous, and seemingly carefree, but nevertheless also dedicated to safety.

They were both auto mechanics, working at a Chevrolet automobile dealership on the northwest side, and both had graduated from the Curtiss Wright Flying Service, a predecessor to the school I was attending, which was operated by Ken Burroughs and a Canadian named L. M. Churback. Coffey and Robinson had submitted their applications to receive training in aircraft maintenance and had been accepted. But when they first presented themselves at the school, where it was obvious they were black, they were refused permission to register. They returned to work and told their boss, Emil Mack, who encouraged them not to drop out of the school. He advised them to tell the school administrators that if they refused to admit the two, they would be faced with a substantial lawsuit.

Coffey and Robinson were therefore admitted, reluctantly, and warned that, as the only blacks enrolled, they would meet some opposition, as there were students from a number of Southern states. Sure enough, they were pushed out of line when they went to get tools and even on their breaks when they tried to buy soft drinks. Their instructor noticed all this behavior, and one night he lectured the white students on Coffey's and Robinson's achievements and the fact that they owned their own plane. Attitudes changed, and the two graduated with high honors.

Churback told them they could instruct other black students if they recruited enough of them for a class, so the men canvassed the neighborhoods of the South Side to urge blacks to get into aviation, whether as airplane mechanics or pilots. By the time I enrolled, on Tuesday and Thursday evenings, Coffey and Robinson both were licensed pilots. Both taught all of the subjects necessary for us to graduate from ground school. I was the first woman in the class. The men probably thought I soon would drop out, but they were wrong. I was tenacious, as usual. As my father had said, "If Jack can do it, so can Jill." We all did very well, especially in the first projects. Eventually there were 27 students in my class, all of us black. Six were women: Dorothy Weaver, Doris Murphy, Willa Brown, Lola Jones, Marie St. Clair, and me.

Our class was well educated and eager, anxious to learn all we could during the winter months so that when warmer weather came we actually could learn to fly. First, though, we had to learn aerodynamics, navigation, and civil air regulations, as well as meteorology. All of the women, except Willa Brown and me, dropped out, or at least didn't continue with the program. Willa later married Coffey, with whom she operated a Civilian Pilot Training Program (CPTP) flight school; she also was an officer in Coffey's Civil Air Patrol (CAP) squadron, the first black officers in the Illinois wing of the CAP.

After meteorology, in which we learned that clouds were not slushy snow but a real danger to pilots, especially when towering cumulus clouds could be followed by a violent summer storm, we studied navigation. With no road signs in the skies, we had to learn how to get from one place to another and back to where we started, using both road maps and aeronautical charts. Then there were the rules and regulations to learn, and aerodynamics. Parts of the airplane, and how each worked with the other to keep us in the air, brought new terms which, I think, we all learned easily because already we had become dedicated.

Coffey also taught us about how airplanes are put together, what makes the engine run, and how to check each part of the airplane to assure it is safe to fly. Coffey was one of the first blacks licensed by the federal government as an aviation mechanic and was not about to let our ignorance reflect badly on his good name. We learned. The training has remained invaluable to me—I still am not afraid to use tools for home repairs.

We all wore white coveralls in our aircraft maintenance classes with Coffey, because the engines were dirty. Perhaps not dirty to a mechanic, but to us oil and grease were dirty. At first I didn't know one wrench from another. The school had a lot of different tools, but sometimes there were not enough to go around. So I conferred with Coffey and he told me what I needed; then I went over to Sears and bought my own, with a shiny green toolbox to keep them in. I kept those tools for years and still have a pair of pliers, a couple of wrenches, and a screwdriver from that old kit.

We made model airplanes, too, and were just like children, tossing those planes across the room. All of us who completed the course passed the year-long ground-school course, earning a certificate attesting to our knowledge.

One day I asked Coffey, "When are we going to do some real flying? When are we going to get in an airplane and fly?" The school had no planes, so I decided to go out on my own. Coffey took me out to Acres Field in Melrose Park, where he and Robinson lived and kept their plane, and introduced me to a friend, a white fellow named "Dynamite" Anderson, and I was able to take some lessons with him in a Travel Air. He was a good instructor, as well as a good friend of Coffey's. I paid $15 an hour, a lot of money in those days, but I was determined to start learning to fly.

Our whole Aeronautical University class was so enthusiastic about the prospect of flying that we formed the Challenger Aero Club, organized by Coffey and Robinson. It turned out to be auspicious because, in a way, we had to build our own airport. In those days, blacks usually were banned from airports for white flyers, though there were occasional exceptions. Coffey and Robinson met with the mayor of Robbins, Illinois, an all-black community just south of Chicago, and talked with him about using some vacant land for an airport. The mayor gave his approval, but we had to supply all the time, labor, and materials. The land had to be leveled, trees cut down, rocks moved, and ditches filled for a northeast-southwest runway. There wasn't room for more than one runway, and, anyway, the prevailing winds were mostly from the southwest.

Every Saturday, Sunday, and holiday we met in Robbins to work. I often took lunch for everyone: hot dogs, which we cooked over a fire, potato salad, lemonade or pop. Sometimes our Robbins neighbors helped with the work; at times it seemed like we had help from the whole little village. Albert Cosby, one of our club members, used his truck to haul cinders from a railroad yard. We used the cinders, the residue from coal burned by steam locomotives of the period, for the runway; these had to be spread, leveled, and tamped down. As I remember, Cosby's truck often would go only in reverse! It was back-breaking work, but we all enjoyed it.

Toward the end of summer, it occurred to us that we didn't have an airplane for our new airport so, with advice from Coffey and Robinson, I bought a used airplane, an International with a Curtiss OX-5 90-horsepower engine, from a man named Freitag. I didn't even see the plane first, for which I think I paid $500, because I trusted Coffey and Robinson. It was a biplane, painted red, with two open cockpits and the barest of instrumentation. I think there were only a compass, an altimeter, and a tachometer. The fuselage framework was wood, covered with fabric. The front cockpit could hold two and the rear one. It did have dual controls, and solo flight was normally done from the rear seat. The wing span was 35 feet, and the fuselage was around 25 feet long. Fully loaded, it weighed 2,100 pounds, about as much as today's Cessna 172 or Piper Cherokee 140.

It was a glorious day when Coffey and Robinson flew my plane to our new airport, but it also was getting cold, the end of the summer flying season. We would have to wait through the winter before we actually could learn to fly. Because that winter was so inclement, with much snow and very cold, the plane sat for months—it seemed longer than that, so anxious was I to take more flying lessons—in the hangar we had built. Coffey frequently would start the engine and rev it up just to make sure it was working properly.

The next spring, in 1934, I finally really learned to fly.* We started out in full force with my airplane. Coffey was one of my instructors.

---

*In the appendix to William J. Powell's 1934 book *Black Wings,* Janet Harmon Bragg, then Janet Harmon Waterford, is listed as holding an industrial license as of December 31, 1932, according to information Powell reportedly obtained from U.S. Department of Commerce records. The industrial license was a subcategory of the commercial license (probably a step along the way) but was eliminated as a category by the time the Civil Aeronautics Act of 1938 was enacted.—*Ed.*

He was very patient, emphasizing everything important, using a lot of hand motions. To illustrate something, he would clear a spot on the ground with his shoe, then draw a chart of what I should do. You didn't forget what he told you. He was an excellent instructor, as well as a master mechanic.

You could put your dollar on it that the OX-5 engine was in good condition and the plane airworthy. I soloed after ten hours of instruction, as did the ten others now left in the club. Grover Nash, a Dunbar Vocational School teacher who was the first black to fly the U.S. mail, later becoming a flight instructor, and Harold Hurd, who worked for the *Chicago Defender* newspaper and was the first to solo, were two of them. Nash also took flight lessons from Roscoe Turner, the famous racing pilot who won the Thompson Trophy three times. Because I could pick my work hours, I could fly almost every good-weather day.

We were instructed to climb to 800 or 1,000 feet and fly a pattern around the airport. We all did it in my plane. Sometimes, I think everyone else got more out of it than I did. While our runway was usable, it was also fairly short, so we barely got off the ground in time to clear the houses bordering the field, no matter in which direction we took off. Our white neighbors to the south, in Midlothian, really didn't like our flying so low over their homes, and often complained. I didn't blame them.

Eventually I was ready for my first cross-country flight. As usual, I was wearing my flying togs—leather helmet and goggles, leather jacket, riding breeches and boots. Women didn't wear slacks in those days, so riding breeches became flying breeches, a sort of uniform. I took off nicely, with Coffey watching from the ground, and flew to Joliet, then to South Chicago, and back to Robbins. As aeronautical charts were nowhere near as good as they are today, and because I was flying fairly low, I supplemented them with road maps. Much of the time I followed railroad tracks, which proliferated in that area. I was well prepared, though, and had no fear of getting lost during the three-hour flight.

Finally, with thirty-five solo hours, I was ready to take the test for a private pilot's license. In a rented plane, Johnny Robinson accompanied me to Pal-Waukee Airport, north of the city, where I took the test and passed with no problems. The federal examiner, a very nice white man, said, "It doesn't matter what color you are, just that you know what you are doing." With the good instruction I had received, I did.

The small hangar we had built at Robbins, which was difficult to get my plane in and out of because of the supports we put in, was blown down during a storm the next year. Fortunately, John Robinson had made arrangements with the white-run Harlem Airport on Harlem Avenue in Oak Lawn, another southern suburb, to use a small area on the south side of their field. We erected a small building as our club's headquarters. It was a new beginning—an airport with much better runway lengths. Nash had bought a Buhl Pup, so now we had two planes. At Harlem we changed the name of the club to the Challenger Air Pilots' Association, but most of us continued to use the old name for some time.

Coffey and Robinson decided to fly to Tuskegee Institute in Alabama for Robinson's tenth class reunion. They hoped to persuade the faculty to start a flying school, with students learning to fly but also taking regular Tuskegee courses. They crashed their OX-6 powered International en route in Decatur, Alabama. Nash had been flying along with them in his new single-seat Buhl Pup and lent it to Robinson, who continued on to Tuskegee but didn't succeed in talking officials into the school. Later, of course, during World War II, Tuskegee had one of the most famous aviation schools, part of the government's Civilian Pilot Training Program, turning out a multitude of fine black pilots.

Fortunately, no one was injured in the crash. After his return to Chicago, Robinson bought a Commandaire biplane and we continued flying.

In 1935 Robinson offered his services to Ethiopian Emperor Haile Selassie, whose country expected an invasion by Italy. Robinson became head of the Ethiopian air force in a relatively short time. He instructed many natives in aviation technology (including flying), and even flew the emperor himself, but returned when the invasion occurred. Coffey, who stayed behind to collect equipment, missed going to Ethiopia because of the invasion. Robinson escaped to Paris, where he cabled Coffey for money to return to the States. Coffey didn't have the cash, so he sold his plane to raise money for Robinson's fare home.

After his return from Ethiopia, Robinson organized his own flight school in 1936, located in the coach house behind Poro College for beauticians, operated by Anna Malone. Coffey sometimes taught evening classes there, continuing with his own flight instructions at Harlem Airport. Robinson, Walter Murray (a student), and I flew south in Robinson's gull-wing Stinson on a recruitment trip for the school. We had a forced landing in western Tennessee, but no one was injured and the plane was not damaged. The four-day flight created considerable interest among potential black students.

In 1944 Robinson returned to Ethiopia with six mechanics, but Coffey could not go because by then he had contracted to operate a Civilian Pilot Training Program flight school. Robinson crashed a plane in Ethiopia and was seriously injured. Shortly afterward he died there of pneumonia, a complication of his injuries.

While at Harlem Airport in the mid-'30s, I bought a brand-new Piper Cub in the traditional yellow, with a bear cub depicted on the tail. It was a cabin plane, a three-place aircraft with dual controls. It had a two-way radio, which was something special at that time. As I had purchased it from a Mr. Zimmerman, who was in the insurance business, my monthly payments included good insurance. I used this plane mostly for myself, though Harold Hurd and Grover Nash also flew it, as I needed help in keeping it up. They were the only ones I really trusted to fly it safely. Coffey also bought a plane, so with Nash's Buhl Pup and my Cub we had three aircraft. Nash started using my Cub for flight instructions and paid me for its use.

After I earned my license, I flew to Atlanta for a Graduate Nurses Association conference. I took William Wells, a pilot and very good mechanic, and his wife, Dorothy, with me, so he could help me fly the long distance and also assure that my Piper Cub stayed in good condition. We landed first at Owens, Kentucky, for fuel, then took off for Chandler Field in Atlanta. Coming in for a landing, I called on the two-way radio for approach procedures. This was the period before many airports had air traffic controllers, so it probably was the airport operator who told me to drop down to 600 feet, then 400 feet, and then brought me right on down to runway 1, in front of the hangars. He knew it was a woman's voice on the radio, but not whether I was black or white. When he saw me climb out of the Cub he was so surprised he was speechless.

I asked a black line-maintenance man about hangar space. "Let me go in and see," he replied. He came back as I was canceling my flight plan. The white man in charge said there was no room, but the black man piped up, "Oh yes, there is; there's space" (where someone had flown out). I asked for his name, which he said was Mose, and I gave him $5 to "take care of my baby."

It was like old-home week being back at my school-days stamping ground in Atlanta. The other nurses were very impressed to find I'd flown my own plane all the way down from Chicago. After attending some of the functions during the three-day meeting, we headed back for Chicago, stopping in Nashville for fuel. The weather was good both ways, so each leg took only one day's flying time, albeit a long day. I couldn't have done it by myself and was most grateful for Wells's help and his wife's company.

My mother, who had been living with me, didn't know anything about my flying until a friend of hers read about "The Flying Nurse" in the *Chicago Defender* and told her. Well, one fine day I took her to Harlem Airport to allay her fears and show her my new Piper.

"Just get in," I told her. "If you don't like it, we won't take off." She climbed aboard with some difficulty, I buckled her in, then taxied down the runway, waiting for her decision.

"If anything happened to you, I'd die anyway," she said, so I took off, circling the field. Mother held on tight to her seat. After a while she liked it. "It was just beautiful, really beautiful," she said on landing. Mother called all her friends on the telephone and told them she had flown "almost to heaven." In fact, she became so enthusiastic she said she would fly down to St. Louis to visit relatives. I wasn't ready for that.

4

The Civilian Pilot Training Program

> We had to make everyone understand that aeronautics
> was a science, like medicine, and that someone could
> specialize in whatever part of the airplane he or she
> wanted to. We needed trained mechanics and
> instrument technicians, and if we didn't have these
> qualified techs we would not have pilots.

My colleagues in the Challenger Air Pilots' Association and I were
elated when the government announced the Civilian Pilot Training
Program (CPTP) in 1939. This would be our opportunity to obtain
advanced training and certificates without it costing us anything. At
any time, learning to fly can be expensive. Our elation turned to
depression when we learned CPTP was to be limited only to white
students. That was just too much to take. We all had paid dearly, in
cash and effort, to get where we were as pilots and we knew from practical experience that we were just as able and expert as any white pilot.

We had learned at an early stage that it took money, and plenty of
it, to stay in the field of aviation. We had established a solid foundation by now, and we had to keep building. We were climbing
"Jacob's Ladder," and every rung took us higher and higher.

To combat what we thought was unfair treatment by the government, we organized the National Airmen's Association of America (NAAA) "to further stimulate interest in aviation and to bring about a better understanding in the entire field of aeronautics," according to our state charter. We held our first meeting, and many others, at the all-black Wabash Avenue YMCA at 3763 South Wabash Avenue. No member missed a meeting. All of us were dreamers, and we knew that one day our dreams would crystallize into reality. I was a charter member, along with Cornelius Coffey, Dale White, Harold Hurd, Willa Brown, Marie St. Clair, Charles Johnson, Chauncey Spencer, Grover Nash, Edward Johnson, George Williams, and Enoch P. Waters Jr. We were incorporated by the state of Illinois on August 16, 1939, with Coffey as president.

Our main objective was to stimulate interest in aviation and to bring about a better understanding in the entire field of aeronautics for blacks. We had to make everyone understand that aeronautics was a science, like medicine, and that someone could specialize in whatever part of the airplane he or she wanted to. We needed trained mechanics and instrument technicians, and if we didn't have these qualified techs we would not have pilots.

With this basic aim and a dogged determination, the NAAA decided to send representatives on a flight across the United States to visit black colleges and universities, to inform the students about opportunities in aviation, to describe all the goodies they were missing because they were not showing enough interest in aviation.

The NAAA appealed to the U.S. government, federal officials in the administration, and Congress, asking that, as U.S. citizens, blacks be included in the aviation training programs then beginning. Enoch P. Waters, one of our NAAA members and city editor of the *Chicago Defender* newspaper, was interested in our problem and became our advisor. He suggested that it could be very valuable for a couple of flyers from the NAAA to fly to Washington, D.C., and visit congressional representatives, whom he would contact personally, and then also visit officials at the city, county, and state level. We "knew our rights," or at least we knew we wanted to learn more about flying, and we knew the CPTP was the way to do it.

We selected Chauncey Spencer and Dale White, both very handsome and very intelligent. They both were from the Works Progress Administration (the WPA). Dale was the conservative type, while Chauncey was just the opposite, an outgoing personality. They made a perfect team. We were proud of them and glad to have them represent us.

Financing the flights was our next hurdle. We had to rent a plane for Dale and Chauncey. We found a Lincoln-Paige biplane owned by Art La Toure, but the rental was $500. Chauncey had saved $500, which he committed to the flight, but what about fuel, hotel expenses, food, and incidentals? They needed a minimum of $2,000. Mission impossible? Heck, no! All our NAAA members drained their pockets. Chauncey, with tears in his eyes, told one of his coworkers, Queenie Davis, his sad, sad story, that we didn't have enough money. Queenie, a very charming lady with all the answers, listened. Knowing Chauncey, I'm sure she had tears in her eyes when he finished talking with her. She suggested we contact the Jones brothers, Ed and George, who then headed the "policy racket"* in Chicago and also owned the Ben Franklin store at 47th Street and South Parkway. The Jones brothers gave us the needed money. Mission possible.

Chauncey and Dale were given a rousing sendoff from Harlem Airport for their flight east to Washington on May 9, 1939. After three or four hours in the air, they were forced down in Sherwood, Ohio, with a broken crankshaft. Coffey, president of NAAA and the backbone of our group, drove to Ohio and repaired the plane. After a few days' delay and several stops, they arrived in the capital. Then they began their talks with government officials and others interested in our cause. Fortunately, all of our efforts, and theirs, proved fruit-

---

*Policy rackets were a kind of numbers game: people bet on a combination of numbers, like a lottery, and won based on their numbers showing up on pieces of paper called "policy slips."—*Ed.*

ful. Even in those days there were blacks who had power and influence, and there were whites who were willing to help us in our progress toward equal opportunity in aviation.

Despite the fact that those lined up for our plea were people of considerable local influence—officials like Chicago Mayor Edward J. Kelly and Illinois Governor Dwight H. Green, with senators and congressmen from Illinois, including Rep. Everett McKinley Dirksen, and Edgar G. Brown, president of a government employees union—the most important person was encountered by accident. He was Sen. Harry S Truman, whom they met while with Brown, as they departed from the electric car which runs underground from the Capitol to the congressional office buildings. After Brown's introduction, Dale and Chauncey explained to Senator Truman that they had flown to Washington from Chicago to get approval for an appropriation which would include blacks in the CPTP. Senator Truman said he could not understand why blacks were not included in the program or why blacks were not admitted to the U.S. Army Air Corps. Truman, being from Missouri (the "show-me" state), wanted to see the plane and made arrangements to go to the airport that afternoon to look at the Lincoln-Paige. When he saw the old plane he was amazed and said, according to Chauncey, "If you had guts enough to fly this trip to Washington, I've got guts enough to see that you get what you are asking for."

Truman gained the backing of President Franklin D. Roosevelt and Representative Dirksen, along with that of First Lady Eleanor Roosevelt, Mary McLeod Bethune, director of Negro Affairs for the National Youth Administration, and others. The president reportedly said, "The changing world conditions outside the American hemisphere make it imperative for the United States to take immediate steps for the protection of the liberties and pursuits of all its citizens."

The trip was therefore successful, and through our efforts blacks were able to participate in the Civilian Pilot Training Program, even though it was in "civilian aviation schools which shall be designated by the CAA (Civil Aeronautics Authority) for the training of Negro air pilots."* I'm very proud to have participated in the first program which enabled blacks to learn to fly on a larger scale.

The First Lady visited Tuskegee after the program was in operation and went flying with Charles Alfred "Chief" Anderson, then and now the nation's best-known black flight instructor. Was this not proof enough that blacks could fly?

On their way back to Chicago, Chauncey and Dale made stops at schools and colleges to promote aviation and thus help protect the safety of the United States and its allies. This cross-country trek was a much greater success than we had planned, or even hoped for. Later, during his fight for reelection in 1948, Truman said, "in giving Negroes the rights that are theirs, we are only acting in accordance with our ideals of true democracy."

At this writing, there are eight NAAA members still alive. It is a great feeling, a proud one, that we played a concrete part in aviation and have been active up to now. It's a glorious feeling.

The Coffey School of Aeronautics at Harlem Airport became the first and only black non-college CPTP school. Pilots who completed basic training at Harlem were sent down to Tuskegee for advanced training. Later, many of us who flew at Harlem became members of an all-black Civil Air Patrol squadron, with Coffey and Willa Brown as its leaders.

Because there were some would-be pilots ineligible for one reason or another—usually because they were too old to enter Coffey's CPTP school—Charles Johnson and I established another flight school at Harlem. He had two planes, both Piper Cubs, and I had my Piper Cruiser, so we were well equipped. Chicago's winter weather, however, made it difficult to fly when there was snow on the ground, as in those days runways were not plowed and, anyway, ours were sod. So once snow time came we did little flying.

---

*This quote is from Patricia Strickland, *The Putt-Putt Air Force: The Story of the Civilian Pilot Training Program and the War Training Service,* Federal Aviation Administration publication GA-20-84.—*Ed.*

Our flight school had several white students, including three women. One day, one of them—I'm sorry I don't remember her name—came to me with an application for the WASPs, the Women's Auxiliary Service Pilots, a group which was ferrying military aircraft across the country, some of them even to England. "I want you to fill this out," she said to me, "and I'm going to see it is mailed, because I'm going to mail it myself."

Well, I did fill it out, and she mailed it. About two weeks later I received a telegram from an Ethel Sheehy, asking me to come to the Palmer House for an interview. When I told the three women about the telegram, which they, too, had received, all of us were elated. We made arrangements to meet at the hotel, but I went down alone.

When he saw me, the black elevator starter at the hotel directed me to a rear elevator—one for servants, although I didn't realize at first what he had done. I pushed the button and saw immediately what kind of elevator it was, so I went back to the starter and told him I had an interview with Mrs. Sheehy, and he apologized.

Mrs. Sheehy had a suite of rooms for the interviews. Two of our women pilots were there already, and one was being interviewed. When it was my turn, I went into the room, and Mrs. Sheehy looked at me and gasped. "Are you Janet Harmon Waterford?" I replied, "Yes." "And do you fly?" she continued, and I said, "Yes." Then she said, "I've never interviewed a colored girl." Mrs. Sheehy didn't know what to say to me, though she did point out that WASP training would be in Sweetwater, Texas, and seemed to feel I would object to that. Finally, she passed the buck, saying she would have to refer my case to Jacqueline Cochran at "headquarters." Eventually I received a telegram from Miss Cochran stating that "whatever Mrs. Sheehy told you still stands." In other words, I was refused because of the color of my skin. After this rejection I was upset. I knew I could fly. I even had my own plane! But this was a defeat, and something I couldn't accept.

I didn't give up. Mother called my attention one morning to a *Chicago Tribune* article asking for 6,000 or more nurses needed for the military nurses corps. She thought it would be safer than flying. I decided to join, but guess what? I was told that "the quota for colored nurses is filled." Now I had made two attempts to serve my country, the only country I knew, and had been refused—not because of any physical or mental condition, but because I was black. At this point I thought I needed a psychiatrist.

I then decided to get my commercial and instrument certificate. I had already completed the theory for a commercial license and passed the written exam, but the uncertainty of Chicago's weather would seriously delay my getting the certificates near home in the winter. I thought, "I will never get them here. What can I do? Where can I go?" I realized I already knew where I needed to go—to Tuskegee, where the weather was more reliable, the Army was teaching black pilots, and there was a CPTP school. And to do that I needed to contact "Chief" Anderson, the head of the CPTP at Tuskegee.

We worked hard and studied hard at the Aeronautical University in Chicago. Cornelius Coffey is in the front row, second from right. John C. Robinson is in the top row, third from left (wearing a business suit). I'm in the top row, fifth from left. (Courtesy Cornelius Coffey and the National Air and Space Museum)

This International model F-17, with a 90-horsepower Curtiss OX-5 eight-cylinder, water-cooled engine, was the kind of airplane I first purchased. (Courtesy National Air and Space Museum)

The members of the Challenger Aero Club (later renamed the Challenger Air Pilots' Association) gather in front of our hangar at Robbins Airport, Robbins, Illinois. We spent several months building the airport and hangar ourselves. I'm near the center, standing next to the small airplane, a Church Midwing. Club president John C. Robinson is at the extreme right. (Courtesy Harold Hurd and the National Air and Space Museum)

John C. Robinson was the founder, along with Cornelius Coffey, of our Challenger Air Pilots' Association. He became famous for flying for the Ethiopian government in its 1936 war with Italy.

Modeling one of my own flying suits for some friends. (Collection of Janet Harmon Bragg)

Challenger Air Pilots' Association members and friends inspect the wreckage of our hangar at Robbins Airport after it and the aircraft in and outside were destroyed by a sudden windstorm in May 1935. (Courtesy Harold Hurd and the National Air and Space Museum)

Members of the Challenger Air Pilots' Association assemble at the church of Reverend J. C. Austin, who helped sponsor our early memorial flights over the grave of Bessie Coleman in Lincoln Cemetery on Chicago's far South Side. I'm in the middle of the second row. (Collection of Janet Harmon Bragg)

Five of the women members of the Challenger Air Pilots' Association pose at Harlem Airport in the early 1930s. Left to right: Lola Jones, Willa Brown, Doris Murphy, me, and Marie St. Claire. (Courtesy Pima Air and Space Museum, Tucson)

Sitting on a fence at Harlem Airport. (Collection of Janet Harmon Bragg)

This is the office and operations building for the Johnson Flying Service that Charles "Pops" Johnson and I ran at Harlem Airport in the early 1940s. We provided flight training for black student pilots and others who were unable to enter the Civilian Pilot Training Program being operated by the Coffey School of Aeronautics, also at Harlem. (Courtesy Pima Air and Space Museum, Tucson)

Cornelius Coffey (second from left) congratulates Dale White and Chauncey Spencer for their successful May 1939 flight from Chicago to Washington, D.C., and back (stopping at several other cities) to demonstrate that African Americans deserved to be included in the Civilian Pilot Training Program. (Courtesy Harold Hurd and the National Air and Space Museum)

The last airplane I owned was a Piper PA-12 Super Cruiser three-seat aircraft like this one, manufactured beginning in 1946. (Courtesy National Air and Space Museum)

I was thrilled to meet Lt. Gen. Benjamin O. Davis Jr. (USAF, Ret.) at the September 1982 opening of the exhibit "Black Wings: The American Black in Aviation" at the National Air and Space Museum. (Courtesy National Air and Space Museum)

The honorees at the opening of the "Black Wings" exhibit included, left to right, C. Alfred "Chief" Anderson, William Thompson, Clyde Hampton, Rufus Hunt, me, Lt. Gen. Benjamin O. Davis Jr., Harold Hurd, and Chauncey Spencer. (Photo by Marjorie M. Kriz, courtesy National Air and Space Museum)

Sharing the podium with Louis Purnell, former member of the all-black World War II 99th Fighter Squadron, and "Chief" Anderson at a National Air and Space Museum program on black aviation history. (Photo by Marjorie M. Kriz, courtesy National Air and Space Museum)

I was reunited in 1985 with "Chief" Anderson and Cornelius Coffey at the annual convention and air show of the Experimental Aircraft Association in Oshkosh, Wisconsin. With us are Paul Bohr, then director of the Federal Aviation Administration's Great Lakes Region, and Adm. Donald Engen, then FAA administrator. (Photo by Marjorie M. Kriz, courtesy National Air and Space Museum)

In 1985 I received the 14th Annual Bishop Wright Air Industry Award, for which I had been nominated by my friend Ida Van Smith, founder of the Ida Van Smith Flight Clubs. (Collection of Janet Harmon Bragg)

5

I Go to Tuskegee

Someone once asked me, "Janet, was it worth all the
strain, frustrations, heartache, embarrassment? Why did
you do it?" I still don't have an answer, but I will say
that every defeat was a challenge from which I profited
in one way or another.

In Chicago I already had met Charles Alfred "Chief" Anderson, head
of the Civilian Pilot Training Program at Tuskegee Institute. During
the winter of 1942–43 I contacted him, and he wrote back. "Dear
Janet: Thanks for your note. I will give you all the assistance I can.
Let me know when you can come down. I hope it will be soon.
Sincerely, (signed) C. A. Anderson."

Anderson is noted for the 1933 and 1934 round-trip, long-distance
cross-country flights he made with Dr. Albert E. Forsythe, the first
such flights. They also conducted the 1934 Pan American Goodwill
Flight, which took them from Miami to Nassau, the first such flight
by a land plane. Later stops included Cuba, Jamaica, Haiti, the Do-
minican Republic, Puerto Rico, the Virgin Islands, Grenada, Trini-
dad, and British Guiana. That was a major achievement for any pilot.

The note from "Chief" was all I needed. I immediately telephoned Anderson and accepted his invitation. I still was employed by the Metropolitan Burial Insurance Association as a health inspector, however, and knew I couldn't leave work without notice. I felt it was important work, too. During the Depression and war years many people did not have enough money to bury members of their families. Some would take up a collection from relatives and friends to help pay funeral expenses, but Metropolitan's policyholders would have all their burial expenses paid: the grave site (mostly in Lincoln Cemetery, where "Brave Bessie" Coleman is buried), the casket, everything was included in a $400 burial then. Although to some $400 might as well have been a million, the company boomed, and it was a godsend to Chicago's poor blacks.

I made an appointment with Robert Cole and Fred Lewing, two of the company officers. I told them I wanted a leave of absence for four to six weeks to go to Tuskegee for advanced flying lessons. They were much impressed and interested, but worried about how I would survive. Really, though, I had not thought of much but getting to Tuskegee. I was willing to spend my last cent for the privilege of flying for "Chief." I told my bosses I had saved a few pennies, not much, and I didn't know how long my nest egg would last.

Mr. Cole remarked, "Don't worry. We will work something out for you." I walked out of the office on the proverbial Cloud Nine. Several days later, I was called into the office again. The two men had discussed my proposed leave with the nursing staff, all of whom had decided to double up, do my work, and send me my check for one month. They gave me gas coupons and sent me off in grand style. That company was like family. The executives showed great interest in the welfare of all the employees. They wanted to see all of us succeed, to have nice homes, cars, whatever made us happy. That meant a lot to us.

Tuskegee, here I come! All preparations were completed for my flight. I left the flight school at Harlem Airport in the capable hands of my partner, Charles Johnson. Walter Robinson, a young flight instructor, Manuella Jackson, a flight student, and I took off from Harlem one cold morning in February 1943, bound for Tuskegee in Charles Johnson's red Piper Cub. Manuella and I wore white coveralls I had designed, rather than the riding breeches, leather jackets, and helmets which were a uniform of sorts both for men and women flying in open cockpit planes of the period. Besides, the Cub had an enclosed cabin.

That first day we flew as far as Nashville and landed at a small airport for the night and for refueling. A young man took us to Fisk University, the famed all-black college, and we spent the night on the campus. The next morning, bright and early, we returned to the airfield, which was near the Cumberland River. The fog was like soup. Visibility was nil. It was not until noon that the fog burned off. The owner of the airfield was not too cordial, and we were getting a little tense at the delay, so we were happy to get clearance and be on our way.

We had a stiff headwind and did not make the time we had hoped. Our fuel was running low. We were trying to get to Huntsville, Alabama, but had to make a forced landing in an open field at Boaz, Alabama. The landing, by Walter, was perfect. Then people started coming, I don't know from where, so many folks and so quickly. We asked where the nearest gas station was—the plane flew on high-octane auto gas. A young white fellow driving a pickup truck had a five-gallon container in the back and drove us to the gas station. At that time we needed coupons to buy gas, but I had plenty of them thanks to the nurses with whom I worked. Mr. Cole had ordered the office to issue me some coupons as well.

It was almost dark, maybe thirty minutes of daylight left. Thinking about spending the night, I asked, very politely, "Are there any colored people living nearby?" There was a young, strong, healthy white lad sitting on a stool at the gas station with a big stick in his hand, striking it on the ground at intervals. He answered my question by saying, "Naw, we are pretty tough on niggers around here." Walter was born in Minnesota, and this was his first experience with Southern "hospitality." He looked at me. I winked at him and gave him a signal not to say anything, for Walter could have popped this guy for his remarks. If he had, we would have been in T-R-O-U-B-L-E.

We went back to the plane, where Manuella had everything under control, answering question after question. She was a Chicago native, and this also was her first trip South. We put gas in the plane, enough to get us to Huntsville, just over the hill and less than five minutes of flight time.

Walter asked, "Janet, are we going to take off?" and I said, "Hell, yes!" for I had decided that a glorified death in an airplane was much better than swinging in the breeze with a rope around our necks like "strange fruit." So we took off over the hill, spotting an emergency landing strip used by Air Corps cadets to refuel. The man in charge, a white civilian, was exceptionally nice when we told him where we were headed. He filled the gas tank—no charge—and we asked him about a place to spend the night.

"Oh yes, ol' James Smith lost his wife a couple of months ago and he has a big house. He's quite lonely. I'm sure he will accommodate you. I will drive you there." We all piled into his truck, and off we went to Jim's house. Jim, who was eating his supper, had enough to share with us and we had a great meal, real Southern cooking: liver and onions, with rice and cabbage, and homemade bread. You would have thought we were long-lost relatives. We spent a comfortable night, and when morning came we found Mr. Smith had prepared one of those down-home country breakfasts for us: ham, scrambled eggs, hot biscuits, honey, coffee, milk. After we finished eating, he drove us back to the plane. This was true Southern hospitality. As we bid him good-bye, Smith would not accept any money. Fortunately, we had left something for him at the house.

There we were in our little putt-putt, ready to take off again. So I took off. The weather was warm, the engine was purring like a kitten. We sang songs, we recited poetry. In other words, we were just plain happy. It was glorious. Then, there it was: Tuskegee. Moton Field and the Tuskegee Army Air Field. We didn't land there because those were used by military pilots for training. Where was Kennedy

Airport, the CPTP field? Oh, there it was. We landed and taxied over to the front apron. "Chief" Anderson came out to greet us and make us welcome. Of course we had to tell him all about our trip.

"Chief" had made reservations for us to stay in Dorothy Hall at Tuskegee Institute. Dorothy Hall is the guest house: many important people have passed through those portals—millionaires, movie stars, and many other celebrities. I was deeply impressed for my first twenty-four hours there. On the second day, Manuella, who was my roommate, and I were going to the dining room for breakfast. On the way, we met another guest by the name of Booth.* I don't remember her first name, but she was a white writer. I guess she was looking for some material to write about, so we entered the dining room and sat down together.

While we were perusing the menu, I felt a tap on my shoulder. I looked up and here stands this dining-hall matron telling me to go to another table. I told her I was quite comfortable where I was sitting. Then she said, "White folks and colored folks don't eat together in Alabama." And I said, "I thought that only occurred in public places, and Dorothy Hall certainly is not a public place. I thought it was private." "I am sorry, but that is the rule here and I wish you would move," she replied.

All of a sudden, Dorothy Hall disappeared. The beauty of the place was gone. It took on a sad look. The old dining-room matron became an ugly ol' witch. It was the first time in my life that I wanted to wring somebody's neck. Why not here? The next moment I felt sorry for her. Manuella and I left the dining room without eating.

Manuella was so confused she went back to our room. I went downstairs and, just as I got to the outer door, an Air Corps cadet squadron passed by, singing the Air Corps song about the "wild blue yonder" and keeping in step as they sang. It was a beautiful sight to me. They looked so happy and proud to be in the Air Corps. As I

---

*This may have been Clare Boothe, later Clare Boothe Luce after she married Henry Luce, editor-in-chief of Time, Inc.—*Ed.*

stood there I almost said aloud, "Do they know what a struggle, what a fight, what insults we have gone through for them to be air cadets, even though on a segregated basis?"

Yes, one day the cream of the crop would fight in air combat. Some would survive and some would not, fighting for their country. My country and every American's country, black and white, fighting for democracy. *What* democracy? Then my thoughts turned to the fellow in Boaz who had said, "We are pretty tough on niggers around here," and the old colored matron in Dorothy Hall who had just embarrassed Manuella and me. I've always wondered why she didn't ask the white woman to move to another table. I realized the woman writer also must have been embarrassed. Was it worth all this stress? I had ambivalent feelings. I was almost ready to pack the airplane and head back to Chicago.

Oh well, I thought, I've gotten over bigger shocks than these. What the heck.

Somewhat calmer, I strolled around the Tuskegee campus. My older sister Viola and three first cousins had attended Tuskegee Institute. I thought about them. Viola had told me so many beautiful things about Tuskegee, and I wasn't about to let a dining-hall matron spoil things for me. I visited George Washington Carver's laboratory; what a great scientist! He had given the world the formula for peanut butter, and many other uses for the lowly peanut and for the sweet potato, which is one of my favorite vegetables. I visited the Booker T. Washington monument and stopped long enough to say a little prayer, thinking about what he had gone through to establish an institution of higher learning for blacks. Those two men will never, ever be forgotten. Then I forgot all about my hurt feelings. Tomorrow would be another day, and it was.

"Chief" Anderson phoned to say he was sending someone to bring me to the airfield. I really was impressed with all the activities there. "Chief" introduced me to the gang, then took me up in the Cub to check my flying ability—and he was very much pleased. We landed and went to his office. Flight instructor George Allen was to work with me. Allen, from Pennsylvania as was "Chief," had flown with "Chief" for a long time. After "Chief" briefed him about my flying, Allen took charge. He made it clear that flying was a serious business with him and that he had no time to waste. I was very happy with this attitude and told him that I, too, had neither time nor money to waste, so that we should get along quite well.

Before I left the airfield, Allen handed me my schedule. Preflight time at 7 A.M. daily included discussions of many air maneuvers. Lazy eights, chandelles, spins—each one would be perfected before we went on to another one. His instruction really became a part of me, not only in flying but in my everyday life. Flying is a technique. If developed properly it always will be useful. After 50 years, I am still using some of it.

Other instructors who flew with me, like Ray Thomas, Perry Young, and John Young III, all were excellent flyers. Ray later went to Liberia to teach flying, and Perry piloted helicopters between Kennedy International Airport and LaGuardia Field, but John Young died at an early age of a heart attack.

Tuskegee, in Macon County, was "dry." The fellows would drive to Uniontown, a small farming community west of Selma, to get their "spirits." If they were caught with whiskey in their cars they were fined heavily. John Young made contact with friends in Columbus, Georgia, about 35 or 40 miles from Tuskegee, to get their liquor, and I would fly down to get it.

I would "hop" passengers, all John's friends, each depositing a fifth in the baggage compartment. After collecting all the whiskey, I would head back to Tuskegee. I was well schooled in case anything went wrong. Before landing, I would watch for either the all-clear signal or a keep-away signal, if someone had put the wrong folks wise. If it were the keep-away signal, I was supposed to fly off and dump the booze. There was a deep pond near the airfield, and my instructions were to drop the whiskey there and not to miss. Fortunately, it was never necessary to dump the bottles, as I don't know how I would have gotten them out of the baggage compartment while flying the plane. I thus gained the title of "The Flying Bootlegger" as well as "The Flying Nurse."

"Chief" Anderson never knew anything about those trips to Columbus, Georgia. "Chief," I want to apologize to you for doing this. The fellows were so kind and helpful to me, I had to show them my appreciation. Forgive me.

Although I had passed the written test for my commercial pilot's certificate in Chicago, the time limit had expired by the time I was now prepared to take my flight test at Tuskegee. I therefore had to go to Birmingham to take the written test again. Allen, my flight instructor, drove me to the bus station and reminded me to go to the rear and take the last seat. He said, "When you fly all the time you forget all of these segregated earthly laws, so be careful." When I got on the bus I followed his instructions and sat in the rear.

After arriving in Birmingham, I went to the office of T. K. Hudson, the federal flight examiner, where I took the test again. In the middle of the test, I got hungry. I told Hudson, and he very kindly sent someone for a sandwich and a soft drink. I passed the test, and the same day I returned to Tuskegee and told everyone the good news. T. K. would notify "Chief" when he would be coming down to give me the flight test.

Every day Allen put me through some really hard flying. "Chief" checked me out, too. It was great. Then the day arrived when "the man" came. It was just after a rain. That afternoon the air was smooth, just like silk. I had been tutored well. Each instructor had taught me Hudson's techniques, the things he surely would test me on. "Papa," the mechanic at the airfield, had the plane in tip-top shape.

Hudson and I donned parachutes, required then for flight tests, got in the plane, and took off. The first thing he did was to pull a forced landing, just where my instructors said he would. We then climbed up to about 1,200 feet, and I did each maneuver. It all was just as the instructors had told me. It was really beautiful. After each maneuver, Hudson gave me the okay signal with his hand. I really was relaxed.

The plane's performance was magnificent, almost as if the little Piper were saying, "I'll do this flight test myself." Hudson at last gave me the signal to land, and that, too, was perfect, a three-point landing.

My instructors and all the rest came to the plane. They were as happy as I was. "How did she do, Mr. Hudson?" Allen asked. With a long Southern drawl I'll never forget, he answered. "Well, George, she gave me a good flight. I will put her up against any of your flight instructors. But I've never given a colored girl a commercial license, and I don't intend to now." He threw his parachute in his car and drove off.

All of us were shocked, speechless. I looked at "Chief," and tears were in his eyes. Allen was nauseated. The others just walked away, dejected. Finally, I came out of my shocked daze and said, "Don't worry. We will find some way." Every defeat was a challenge.

Despite this disappointment, I enjoyed my visit in Tuskegee. I met so many people, made lasting friends, and was exposed to Army life. I will never forget Lt. Col. Noel Parrish, the base commander at the Tuskegee Army Air Field, where I would fly daily to use the Link trainer. One day, Colonel Parrish sent for me. He greeted me, then said, "Young lady, do you know there is a war on? When you fly your little red plane over here, do you know you are interfering with routine takeoffs and landings? You can cause an accident. I'm sure you don't want that to happen.

"You can make use of the trainer whenever you want," he continued, "but don't fly over here anymore. Is that clear?" He was right, so I couldn't get angry. Instead, after that necessary rake-over, I drove a car whenever I went to the air base.

Parrish, a white Army Air Corps officer, sincerely wanted the training of black pilots to succeed. His attitude increased morale at this unique military base over what it had been under his predecessor. Many of his flight instructors were black.

The air cadets were rascals. They would recognize my plane and fly too close to me. Sometimes I was terribly frightened, but I didn't let them know. "Chief" gave me a job preflighting cadets at the air base.

Nobody sat idle near him. His wife, Gertrude, so kind and sweet, said, "Don't give up, Janet. Stay in there and fight." I did.

While I was at Tuskegee, I flew over to visit my hometown, Griffin, Georgia. My niece E. Jewell Scott was then executive director of the Girl Scouts, black division. She was trying to raise money for her girls, so we had a little air show. My partner's son, Jackie Johnson, who was at Tuskegee as a primary flight instructor, flew over to Griffin and we "hopped" passengers, raising a big sum of money for the Girl Scouts. I was quite a celebrity. "Hometown girl flies home in her own plane, donates all proceeds from an air show to the Girl Scouts" is the way a newspaper headline read. I was very proud to be so recognized, and to be able to help the Girl Scouts.

When I flew back to Chicago in March, after five weeks of hard work mixed with fun and a big disappointment, for some reason I really was happy and confident. After a few days of rest, I flew to Pal-Waukee Airport in a north suburb to try again for my commercial license. I told the flight examiner, Mr. Ritter, a tall Texan, what had happened in Tuskegee. When he spoke with that Texas drawl, I thought, "Oh my God, here we go again."

He said, though, "We shall see." We went up and through some maneuvers like spins, chandelles, lazy eights, the same ones I had done in Alabama. Then he gave the signal to land. I had reached a saturation point. It really didn't make any difference anymore if I passed or failed. But guess what? The man shook my hand, congratulated me, and told me to pick up my license on Wednesday at Chicago Municipal Airport, now Midway Airport. How about those apples!

I wonder now how I could remember so well the whole name of the examiner in Alabama who had refused to pass me only because of my color and sex, and not that of this great man who was interested only in whether I qualified.

Someone once asked me, "Janet, was it worth all the strain, frustrations, heartache, embarrassment? Why did you do it?" I still don't have an answer, but I will say that every defeat was a challenge from which I profited in one way or another.

6

Nursing Homes

The nursing home was a very rewarding experience for
me, particularly after having seen how some old people
lived when I visited homes on insurance business for
Metropolitan. Here they could live in dignity, in
pleasant surroundings, eat well, and have good care.

Everybody at Metropolitan Burial Insurance Association was happy
to see me back and anxious to hear about my adventures. When I
told them about T. K. Hudson, the flight examiner at Tuskegee who
was so biased, they sympathized with me and said, "Don't worry
about it. We're proud of you." Several of my fellow employees had
flown with me earlier and knew how hard I had worked.

After six months of flying at Harlem, the winter of 1943–44 came
all too soon and I could not use my plane much. Grover Nash left to
teach at Chanute Field, and Harold Hurd was in the Air Corps at
Tuskegee. Charles Johnson died, and that was the end of our flight
school. It was time to work for myself.

My brother Pat and I had decided to buy a two-flat apartment
building on the South Side, at 66th Street and Ellis Avenue. He and

his family would live on the first floor, and I would be on the upper floor with my mother. After I had put down $1,000 in earnest money, he changed his mind and I was stuck, because I did not have enough funds for the rest of the down payment. So the man who owned the building took out a second mortgage and sold it to me on contract.

But what to do with the building? My friend Minetta Marian, a registered nurse and nursing home supervisor, who had all the expertise for operating a nursing home, suggested I use the second floor for convalescents. My cousin Frances Moore, an interior decorator, designed and made drapes and bedspreads, and another friend, who worked for Catholic Charities, helped me get used furniture. The beds were painted different colors to match the room walls. It was a beautiful place when we finished.

The result was most attractive, and within weeks I had eight patients, most of them indigents on welfare of some sort. My first month's check from the city of Chicago was $800, the most money I'd had in my hands at one time. The second month's check was over $1,000. Because my work at Metropolitan was mostly in the evenings, when people were at home, or on weekends, I could manage both jobs easily. If any of the patients, all of them ambulatory, needed more medical care they were sent to Cook County Hospital. When I was away, my cousin Sally Batts was on hand as a practical nurse.

As I still was living with my mother at 61st Street and St. Lawrence Avenue, I decided to turn the first floor of the 66th Street apartment into an expanded nursing home. This soon filled up, and my days and evenings were filled with work. Within a short time I had twelve patients, all on welfare. Minetta had told me that welfare patients were best, because the city always paid and money was what I needed at this time. I continued to work at Metropolitan, with my cousins from Georgia, Sally and Pete Batts, helping me in the nursing home. Somehow I still found time for flying, in order to keep my licenses valid and for social and church activities. Later I sold my plane, knowing I always could rent one.

Eventually it became obvious that I should devote more of my time to the nursing-home business. In 1951 I married Sumner Bragg, whom I'd met at Metropolitan, where he was a supervisor. Sumner, a graduate of Fisk University, a four-letter man who had been captain of his football and basketball teams, had majored in sociology and later studied hospital administration at Northwestern University. We had known each other for some time and even dated. My mother thought he was a marvelous man.

In the summer of 1951 my mother became ill, and I brought her to the nursing home for better attention. She died there on October 8, just six weeks before Sumner and I were married. I know she would have been pleased; I wished she could have been there to see how happy we were. We bought a bungalow at 73rd Street and Indiana Avenue and began our new life together.

I resigned from Metropolitan, with regrets as everyone had been so very kind to me over the years. Two years later Sumner and I decided to expand further with purchase of the old Sidney Wanzer mansion at 64th Street and Kimbark Avenue. Wanzer, owner of one of Chicago's best dairies, had moved to "a better neighborhood." I thought the mansion would make a fine nursing home, with room for three times as many patients. But first I had to gain consent from other property owners along the 6400 and 6500 blocks of Kimbark.

Fearing that many property owners, white or black, might not approve, I asked two of my dearest friends—VeNona Roberts Johnson, later a high school principal in Chicago, and Frances Matlock, an outstanding teacher—to talk with each property owner in this changing neighborhood. VeNona and Frances had fun. Both could "pass," so the white owners didn't know of their black ancestry. The white neighbors called the blacks everything they could think of. But my friends had only one purpose: to obtain enough signatures approving turning the empty Wanzer mansion into the Harmon-Bragg nursing home. After 60 percent consented, we began converting the huge mansion.

There was much work to be done. The mansion had to be fire-proofed, with safety exits added. And it had to be redecorated, with furnishings and equipment procured. The Wanzer mansion had twenty-two rooms and three baths on the first and second floors, plus a huge ballroom on the third, along with three servants' rooms and another bath. Any way you looked at it, it was an enormous, rock-solid building, rather Gothic in style, with corner turrets, built both of red brick and stone. It took me two months to fix it up. I hired a painter to make everything fresh and clean, and we painted all the rooms. The downstairs paneling was removed and dumped in the alley for the garbage pickup. That probably was a big mistake; today such paneling is very expensive.

We made a few changes in the bedrooms and the downstairs rooms to be used for convalescents. Some were big enough for four patients, others only for two. The marble baths, very elegant, were fine as is, except we added higher commodes, more suitable for elderly and often infirm people. The rooms were furnished with rosy-beige beds and bedside cabinets bought new from American Hospital Supply Company in Evanston. (This was unlike my first home, whose furnishings were good but secondhand.) My cousin Frances Moore again did the interior decorating, designing each room in a different color. Dishes, tableware, and the like came from a restaurant supply firm. And this time I had to hire much help. A yardman was needed to take care of the outside and the flower garden, and fifteen employees, most of whom I trained myself, to help care for the patients. That was a big job, as none knew the principles of taking care of the elderly and infirm. I also hired another registered nurse. Two of my new employees lived on the third floor in the former servants' rooms, so that someone always was available for extra assistance when needed.

After completion of all requirements to receive a city license, we moved our patients from Ellis Avenue to the new home. Almost overnight the home filled up with the licensed capacity of thirty-five. I made every effort to determine patient compatibility. When I was notified that someone was ready to come in, I would visit that person at the hospital, telling him or her about the home and the other patients. Women were on the second floor, for more privacy, and men on the first.

Before I went to Tuskegee, I had done much private-duty nursing on the side and had made many friends among my patients. One of them, Maurice Dick, owner of the Capital Dairy, gave me six months of free dairy supplies, a wonderful, kind gift.

Sumner joined me in the nursing-home operation after we had acquired the slightly smaller mansion next door, giving us room for sixty patients. We had hoped to build a solarium between the houses, thus connecting them, but never did. Although the new house was smaller, it still was a mansion, with ten large rooms and of similar architectural style. Again we hired a decorator to fix it up so it wouldn't look "institutional." And again the upstairs rooms were large enough for four-bed wards, with smaller numbers in other rooms. We fixed up an office for Sumner in the basement.

I really needed Sumner's help with the nursing home, but he said he didn't like to be among sick people and at first refused. He was a good accountant and had studied sociology in college, backgrounds I needed as the books had to be kept better than I could and the city required a social worker at the home because of the number of patients. Also, fortuitously, Sumner had taken graduate work in hospital administration at Northwestern University. No one but Sumner could fill the job! Finally, after much persuasion, he came into the business with me. We worked well together, and it was he who helped with patient activities.

The nursing home was a very rewarding experience for me, particularly after having seen how some old people lived when I visited homes on insurance business for Metropolitan. I had seen some living on pads on the floor, with insufficient care from their families, often with inadequate food and medical attention. Here they could live in dignity, in pleasant surroundings, eat well, and have good care. As some came to the home with few clothes, I went to a used clothing store to pick up a few things and met the owner. When he learned why I wanted the clothing, he told me to return everything I'd selected to the racks and come back the next day. When I did, he had a couple of huge boxes of good, wearable, washable clothing, for both men and women, which he donated to me. I was very grateful, and so were the patients. I continued to go back to the store to buy things for other patients.

The Board of Health required that we have a menu made up two weeks in advance. While the menu looked good on paper, often the patients did not like the food, even though the meals were well prepared and well balanced. I became tired of "cooking for the garbage can," and asked them, men and women, what they wanted to eat. If what they wanted wasn't harmful I tried to give it to them. One patient, an excellent cook, kept saying, "Why don't you have such and such?" and telling me how to make it. That was a great help. Some of them provided me with recipes I still use today.

We also provided recreation for our patients, but keeping our charges happy was part of the care we gave them. During the summer, we frequently had picnics in the backyard, cooking outside, a welcome change. Church groups came to visit and to take some of their parishioners out to various events. There were weekly craft classes, taught by a woman who instructed patients in crocheting, knitting, making ceramics, macramé. If the teacher didn't show up, then I led the classes. The projects weren't difficult, but the patients did need motivation.

Members of the Ebenezer Baptist Church had a band which played for parties we had on the lawn during warm weather. Nobody would dance, but we could see they wanted to, even though some were in wheelchairs. Church ministers came to call on patients from their congregations and also talked with others. I had to tell one minister to leave and never come back. He was quite dramatic in his preaching, but he was telling my patients they were old and sick because they had sinned. He left them so emotionally disturbed I had to tell him to go. Our staff included a doctor who came when needed or when a new patient needed a special diet set. Medical specialists also visited. If a patient became too ill for us to care for, he or she was sent to Cook County Hospital.

My biggest problem was my employees, not the patients. Mothers on Aid to Dependent Children, after I had expended much time and labor training them as nurses' aides, would decide they could make more money staying home and having more children. Others would steal anything not nailed down. Both problems were not uncommon in such homes. A few of my employees were student nurses who needed this experience to continue in their careers.

At first, I had colored linens to match the room wall colors, so that I could know which went where. Thefts, and a laundress who put so many items in the washing machine that the equipment always was breaking down, ended this nicety and I resorted to a linen service which supplied clean white linens daily. That, of course, didn't end the thefts of sheets, pillowcases, blankets, and towels. It seemed like I always was replacing something. Food also was stolen, even though I bought in cans too large for the average family. One night, driving up with the headlights on, I saw a package in the driveway and discovered someone had surreptitiously left food outside to be picked up, but that I had arrived before that could happen. Firing such employees was a necessity, but replacing them required extra work for me and everyone else. My other major problem was employee tardiness, failure to arrive on time to relieve someone on a shift. Too much of that, and I had to look for someone else.

Fortunately, the patients were happy, at least as happy as one could be living with precarious health. Neighbors and neighborhood church members volunteered their time to talk with patients, read to them, write letters for them. Some of the patients had no families and thus no visitors and no mail. They were the ones we had to do something extra for. You can't just sit all day doing nothing, so the craft classes were an advantage.

We worked hard and were successful, but most of all it was enriching. Twenty-five years of hard work and long hours, plus successful investments, brought Sumner and me a financial position where we could retire, which we did in 1972. We had the houses torn down as they were too big for a modern family and we didn't want to sell them as a nursing home. (I still own the two lots.) We moved from a bungalow to a twenty-first-floor apartment on Lake Michigan across from the Museum of Science and Industry. On a clear day, we could look across the lake to the Indiana dunes where Octave Chanute made his glider experiments in the 1890s.

We also bought a house in Tucson because Sumner's arthritis gradually had worsened and he needed warmer winters. But not to sit and vegetate! Many of our friends had moved to Tucson from Chicago, and we made more. And I entered into new projects which benefited from my experiences as a nursing-home entrepreneur and as a pilot.

While I no longer work as a professional nurse, my experience and training have enabled me to care better for my husband and myself. I'm still a member of the graduate nurses group I joined when I first came to Chicago, and I participate in such of their events as I can when I am in the city. I gave my patients my best, and I know they appreciated it because I stayed in touch with some, and some employees, too, for many years. Who could ask for more?

7

African Students

> I think I saw thirty-five or more graduations with these
> boys. When I look through my scrapbooks, seeing their
> photographs, I remember how good those days were.
> Many of them flew with me in my Piper Cub, the first
> time they had flown in a small plane.

Back in 1936, after John Robinson had returned from Ethiopia,
where he had been training the emperor's air force, things were not
the same at Harlem Airport. Cornelius Coffey and Robinson were
never so close again, probably because Coffey thought Robinson had
abandoned teaching American blacks to fly. Robinson bought a
Stinson, but never offered it to me to fly.

Later, after World War II, Emperor Haile Selassie, finding on his
return from exile that most of the educated Ethiopians had been mas-
sacred by the Italians during their occupation of his country, made
arrangements for likely students to study abroad. Robinson, back in
Ethiopia on his second trip checking air force planes for airworthi-
ness, told two of those students, scheduled to study at Illinois
Wesleyan University in Bloomington, to look me up on arriving in

Chicago. He gave them grimy little notes of introduction as they were leaving Addis Ababa, the capital. He obtained their promise that they would, at least, stop long enough to meet me. That was in 1947, before I married Sumner.

Johnny's description of me must have been enthusiastic. One of his friends sent a telegram from New York telling me when they would arrive, and I met them at Union Station, where they gave me the note, which said, "Take care of these boys like they were your own."

Seifu Selleke and Nerayo Assayus were only the first of more than a hundred Ethiopian students who studied in the United States and became part of my extended family. Seifu and Nerayo called me "Sister." Then I was still young enough to be something of a big sister to them, and the name stuck; students coming later also called me "Sister."

After Seifu and Nerayo, others came, always in twos and threes so they would have a back-home friend nearby. All of them had been given my address and telephone number by those students who had returned home, so that sometimes I had as many as ten or fifteen staying with me over Christmas, other holidays, and vacations. They all had sleeping bags, so there was no problem with not enough beds. They were not only happy to see me but to see each other, as they went to different colleges and universities. Sometimes there were so many that my brother Pat, who then lived in the apartment downstairs, was called upon to provide room. The boys called him "Pops."

Like some other Africans, these young men had never been exposed to segregation, so that many times it was very hard for Seifu and Nerayo, the first to arrive, to understand life in the United States. While at Wesleyan Seifu had a toothache; the university made an appointment and sent him to a local dentist, who just let him sit while he took care of his white patients. Finally the dentist told the young man to return after dark. When he did, before Seifu even sat in the chair, he pulled the shades so no one would know he was treating a black boy. When Seifu called to tell me what had happened, I ordered him to come to Chicago, where he could be cared for properly. The next weekend I took him to my dentist, who did the necessary work, and Seifu went back to school with a different viewpoint.

Problems continued in Bloomington, Illinois, however. When Seifu and Nerayo went with several white student friends to a local skating rink, they were refused admission. I was furious when I heard about this. Nerayo wrote to Illinois Governor Dwight H. Green, stating that he was a guest in the United States and had been insulted. The governor immediately investigated, and the skating rink no longer kept dark-skinned students from using the facilities. Nerayo, who later became a lawyer, knew even at that age that writing the governor would get action.

I drove down to Bloomington for their graduation, which was beautiful. I was very proud that I could help to keep them in school and could guide them. I told them that, in spite of the pitfalls and the hurts, they should remember they came to the United States for an education and that was number one on their lists. Soon they would be going back home to influence other Ethiopians.

Both young men continued their educations in the United States. Nerayo went to graduate school at the University of Illinois to study international law. Seifu, who could not get into medical school because of quotas limiting the number of black students, entered Northwestern University for a master's degree in public health. He was accepted as an intern in public health at Tulane University in New Orleans but was refused admittance after he got there because of his color. In Puerto Rico he found he could work as an intern, but that he would need to learn Spanish. As he was an outstanding language scholar anyway, it didn't take him long to speak adequate Spanish, adding that to French, Italian, English, and his native Amharic. Quite an accomplishment for one his age.

After returning home, Seifu became an organizer for World Health Organization clinics in East and West Africa. Later he operated his own pest control business quite successfully until the Selassie government fell in 1974. At this writing, he lives in Tanzania with his wife, two children, and a grandchild, and works in an official capacity with the World Council of Churches. Nerayo completed his law degree at the University of Illinois in Champaign, then for a time joined a law firm in Chicago before returning home, where he was appointed deputy attorney general by Emperor Haile Selassie. Unfortunately, his promising career was cut short. He died of leukemia in England, where he had gone for treatment.

Alle Felege Selam, another of my students, graduated from the School of the Art Institute of Chicago and Roosevelt University. He had been selected by his government to come to the United States based on his artistic abilities. On arriving in Chicago he went to the old YMCA Hotel on Wabash Avenue because he had misplaced my address and telephone number. Then he went to a white barbershop nearby for a haircut. The first barber left him looking like he had rolls of hair on his head. When he objected, another tried to remedy the effect, which resulted in a patchy hairdo and an unhappy boy. Very frustrated, Alle reported his problem to a passing policeman, who could see this wasn't a proper haircut and told the barbers to do the right thing by the boy. He had very little hair left when they finished.

Alle soon found my address and telephone number and came to live with me and my mother until school started. His frustrations continued at the Art Institute, however, as his art instructor paid little or no attention to his work. When he told me of the neglect, I went to the school and talked with his instructor, telling him Alle deserved to have his work evaluated, just the same as the rest of the students. The situation changed, and Alle finished at the Art Institute with high marks, as well as good grades at Roosevelt.

Back in Ethiopia, Alle painted the domed ceiling of the chief Coptic church and murals for Africa Hall, the United Nations building in Addis Ababa. After that he opened an art school, giving scholarships to many deserving Ethiopian students. His reputation as an artist was such that he was selected to do a statue of a royal ancestor, a project never completed because of the fall of the Selassie government.

Before that, however, Alle returned to the United States as a guest of the State Department, representing artists in Ethiopia. On a visit to the Art Institute he again met the instructor who had ignored him. This time the man invited him to his home for dinner, but Alle declined the invitation because "I have to dine with my sister"—meaning me. I told him he shouldn't have done that, but he said he should, and we laughed about it. He wasn't the little student anymore, he was a big shot, a diplomat.

In the early 1980s Alle sent me his 18-year-old son for a visit so I could talk with him before he went to Texas Tech University at Lubbock. Young Teodros, like his father, was an artist. When I first saw him, he had a huge Afro haircut standing out about a foot all around his head. I said, "Tomorrow we're going to the barbershop so you can get a haircut like your father's" (but not like that first one when he was almost skinned). The barber took off layers, one at a time, until he got what I considered the right length. Teodros was satisfied with it and not unhappy about losing all the hair he had grown while going to school in Frankfurt, Germany. He was my first "grandchild."

We visited the Art Institute, meeting some of his father's instructors, and then went on to other Chicago landmarks Alle had said his son must see. Teodros stayed with me a couple of weeks, and we had lots of fun. His cousin Zewditu Haile, whom I had brought to the United States, was living in Lubbock with her husband, Muleneh Azene, who was working on his Ph.D. in engineering. Muleneh got Teodros a scholarship at Texas Tech, where he seemed to be happy and doing well, we thought, until one day Zewditu called to say Teodros had committed suicide by jumping out of a window. There was talk of foul play, but I never heard any more about it. It was very sad. He was such a sweet boy.

Teodros had known how much I liked birds, and he painted a number of beautiful pictures which I have hanging on the walls of my home in Tucson. I think of him often.

Mulatu Debebe was another student for whom I had to go to bat. He was attending a Bible school in Minnesota, but he didn't like the subjects he was taking. I asked if he wanted me to come up and talk with his instructors, but he said no, that what he really wanted was to go to a technical school. I called a friend in Chicago, Clifford Campbell, principal of Dunbar Vocational School, who arranged for him to enroll at Lewis Institute. I told Mulatu not to mention his impending transfer until it was complete, as the Bible school might try to make him stay because he was on a student visa. He asked me what he should say if he were offered the subjects he wanted, and I told him to say "Forget it."

He later reported, "They told me verbatim what you said they would, and I did what you told me and said 'Forget it.'" He loved his studies at Lewis. After graduation he went home but was unable to use his technical expertise. He became a part of the government, serving at one time as chairman of protocol. He was really well prepared for this, though, with his fine manners and ability to meet people.

Before he left Chicago, he said he would have a gold-and-white guest room just for me. I didn't think much about it then, but when I visited his beautiful home on my trip to Ethiopia in 1972, there was the gold-and-white room, just as he had promised. "Nobody has slept in this room yet," he said. "It's just for you."

Within a range of about 100 miles I would visit all the schools where "my" boys were studying, making sure that their progress was good, that their grades were high. I think I saw thirty-five or more graduations with these boys. When I look through my scrapbooks, seeing their photographs, I remember how good those days were. Many of them flew with me in my Piper Cub, the first time they had flown in a small plane. Some had flown to the United States, while others sailed in style on the *Queen Mary,* but none had flown with a black woman pilot in a small plane before, and it was always a thrill for them.

Eventually many Ethiopian students, those who attended nearby colleges and universities, lived in the ballroom of my Kimbark Avenue nursing home and helped out with my patients. In this way we helped each other.

Meanwhile, all of my efforts on behalf of the students were being reported to Emperor Haile Selassie himself, as the young men had come to love me and appreciate my help. In 1954, when the emperor came to the United States on a diplomatic visit, I received a telephone call from the embassy in Washington about meeting him. The caller, an educational attaché in charge of all the students in the United States, a Mr. Kassa, said, "His Majesty wishes an audience with you when he comes to Chicago."

Naturally, I was not sure I'd heard him correctly and asked him to repeat. Once I understood it was for real, I said, "Whenever you say." A few days later the Chicago papers were full of stories about visiting royalty. His Majesty stayed at the Drake Hotel, with half a floor reserved for him and his entourage. It was there that I met him.

My first glimpse, though, of the diminutive emperor was at Chicago Midway Airport, then the world's busiest. He and his party arrived in a Lockheed Constellation at the south end of the airport, at the old terminal, where police could provide better security. Haile Selassie was welcomed to the city by Mayor Martin Kennelly and other dignitaries, then escorted to a waiting limousine.

All of the Ethiopian students, about twenty-five of them who were at colleges and universities in the area, and I were there. The students lined up like an honor guard, so that the emperor passed between them. Some of the young men prostrated themselves as Haile Selassie walked by, smiling. At the airport I met Endalkatchew Makonnen, the emperor's interpreter, who complained to one of the students that he and the entourage had been so busy since arriving in the United States that they'd had no time to get haircuts. The students passed the word to me and I said, "I will try to get a barber for you." I don't know why the subject of haircuts for Ethiopians arose so frequently, but I assured Makonnen I would obtain a barber.

That afternoon my rumpus room was turned into a makeshift barbershop. Six of the royal party took turns sitting in one of my chairs while the clipping went on. The conversation centered around food, particularly hamburgers and French fries. With assistance from one of the students, who had been watching the shearing, my husband Sumner went out and bought enough burgers and fries for all, and we ate them in the rumpus room.

Makonnen and I also talked about a church at 37th Street and South Parkway (now Martin Luther King Jr. Drive) where the parishioners, none of them Ethiopians, thought so much of the emperor that they faced east and prayed for him each day. Actually, the emperor already knew about this congregation and earlier had given the group land in his country. The emperor, under heavy guard and with permission from the State Department, made a short visit to the church. It was the only place in Chicago with an Ethiopian flag; since I knew about it, I made arrangements for the flag to be used during the emperor's visit.

The next day several students, my brother Pat, and I were summoned to the Drake Hotel for a reception to meet the emperor. We were met on our arrival by the educational attaché, Mr. Kassa, who announced me for my audience with the emperor. I was escorted into a large suite where the emperor was seated at a desk, wearing a khaki military uniform trimmed in red and gold and with a chest full of medals. He stood up to greet me and said, through an interpreter, that in appreciation of what I had done for Ethiopian students I was invited to visit his country as his guest. Then he presented me with a beautiful, heavy Lalavella cross of pure Ethiopian gold.

It was like a fairy story, receiving such a gift and an invitation from a bona fide emperor. Quite naturally, I said, "Thank you, I'm very happy." In fact, I can say now that I was almost speechless. I told him I would be very happy to come to Ethiopia sometime in the near future, but I had no idea then whether I really would.

Haile Selassie was very small in stature. His eyes were searching, but very kind. He smiled sweetly for each student, and for me, and was very patient. I think that's why he was loved so much.

The emperor talked to each of the students individually, remembering where each had come over to study and what he was studying. He had not forgotten a face, or even what province each came from. The reception, held in one of the hotel's elegant public rooms, was limited to the students, my brother, and me. Hors d'oeuvres and champagne were served. I also was invited with the students to a luncheon hosted by city officials at the Conrad Hilton Hotel.

It was truly one of my life's most memorable moments.

8

I Go to Ethiopia

That first trip to Ethiopia impressed me very much. It
was inspiring to see that a country could be governed by
blacks, and that blacks were those who made the
country successful.

When Emperor Haile Selassie invited me to be his guest in Ethiopia,
I had no idea I ever would go to Africa, though I had thanked him
and accepted his invitation. At the time I wasn't actually excited about
going anywhere in Africa. However, in August 1955, four of "my
children" had completed their college courses and were returning
home, sailing on the *Queen Mary* from New York to Southampton,
England. I helped them gift-shop for their mothers and sisters, helped
them pack their gifts, and talked with them about their aspirations for
careers. One of them asked, "Sister, why don't you go with us on the
Queen Mary?" I replied, "You know, I think I will. It would be fun."

I talked about taking the trip with Sumner, who felt that such a
vacation would do me good and that he would be able to take care
of matters at the nursing home in my absence.

Lemme Frehewhoit, one of the students who had urged me to go, said, "Let's call the embassy in Washington and talk with Kassa, and see if we can make reservations for you to go with us." Lemme called, and Mr. Kassa said, "Fine, I'm so glad she's going," and started making the necessary arrangements. He called back to say only a lower-deck accommodation was available on the *Queen Mary,* as I was booking so late. At the time it didn't make any difference to me, as I'd never been on an oceanliner before.

We left Chicago for New York on a Greyhound bus because the boys had to travel inexpensively and, besides, they wanted to see more of the country. Other students, already in New York, knew we were coming and met us at the bus station. From there we took cabs to the Hudson River dock and boarded the *Queen.* It was the first time I'd seen such a ship. She was so huge I couldn't see the other end. The boys were berthed on one deck and I was on a lower one, sharing a cabin with four young women whose husbands were in the U.S. Army in Europe. Waking up the next morning, I found we already were at sea, as the ship had sailed at dawn.

It was such an enormous ship I didn't know where to turn first. I started to look for Lemme, then gave up and had him paged. When he found me I asked him to come to my deck and showed him how crowded my cabin was. I could hardly move around. He said, "Sister, you waited so long before making up your mind that this is all that was left." While that was true, I thought perhaps the purser could find something else, and Lemme offered to handle a search for a larger cabin.

Lemme told the purser I was en route to Ethiopia as a guest of the emperor, explaining that I had waited awfully late to book passage and the embassy had been able to find only a very small cabin. The purser asked Lemme to bring me to his office, where he told me he had one vacant bed in a cabin occupied by an older lady who was seasick. He pointed out that there were four more days at sea and that the woman might continue to be sick, but I thought, "Anything is better than where I am." That day they moved me into the cabin with Mrs. Lillian Smith, who was English. She was really sick, no doubt about it. I instructed her in some breathing exercises I had learned from a friend who had experience with seasickness. The trick was to take big breaths every time you felt nauseous. I had Mrs. Smith taking such breaths, she recovered, and in the last three days we had a ball. After I returned home I received several notes from her, asking me to visit her in her little town north of London, and thanking me for letting her in on the seasick cure secret. Unfortunately I didn't have an opportunity to accept her invitations.

When news spread around the *Queen Mary* that I was Haile Selassie's guest, everything was different. The captain took time to talk with me, stating, "Anything you want, let me know." He hosted me for dinner at his table. The *Queen Mary* had every recreation imaginable—movies, racing, gambling. I think I participated in everything. I even bought a swimsuit and went swimming in the pool, a pool as big as my yard in Tucson, which is pretty big.

After we landed at Southampton we took the boat train into London, where we stayed at the Ethiopian embassy, a huge mansion in a fashionable part of the city. The next day we boarded a different train for the ferry across the English Channel, then a train to Paris, where we stayed at a beautiful old hotel near the Champs Élysées. I was so tired I went straight to bed. The next day I had breakfast in the hotel, then went out to see the city and do some window shopping, returning in time for dinner. After changing my dress, I went down to the dining room, where the maître d' asked me how long I was staying. "About three days," I replied, after which he told me I would have a permanent table. He paraded me around the room, finally seating me in the very middle.

Paris was so much fun I almost forgot I was on my way to Ethiopia. Flights on Ethiopian Airlines then were available only from Athens and not too frequently, but after four days we started off, flying to Athens on TWA. At the hotel in Paris I had met an Ethiopian woman who had two sons at school in England. She was returning home with one son, who was to take her to Athens. Ethiopian women never traveled alone in those days; they always had a male escort. This woman didn't speak English or any language except her native tongue, Amharic. It was fortunate for me that I'd met her, for her son gave up his seat on the Ethiopian airliner from Athens on condition I take care of his mother. I accepted, even though we would have difficulty communicating. We had fun on the plane, where we played games with the TWA magazine. She pointed to a photo and told me the Amharic word, and I told her the English word. In Athens, where we were to change planes, we found the flight was delayed until the next day. An Ethiopian Airlines representative met us at the airport to explain about the delay and then took us to the Grande-Bretagne Hotel, with a grand view of the Acropolis. My Ethiopian friend and I shared a beautiful room, more like an apartment, that had been reserved for the pilots who had failed to arrive. The bathroom was all tiled in mosaics, with a recessed wall scene of the moon over the city.

After taking a luxurious bubble bath in the huge sunken tub, I dabbed Parisian perfume behind my ears as my fellow traveler rocked back and forth on her bed, apparently upset about the delay. I offered her some of the perfume from my miniature bottle, but she went to her bag and pulled out what looked like a whole quart of Chanel No. 5 and offered me some of hers. I thought she probably was going to bathe in it!

I wanted to go sightseeing, but I don't think my friend understood what I had in mind, so I went alone. The Greek shopkeepers, who apparently had seen few black women, waved at me as I passed by and I waved back.

The next day the plane arrived and we took off, stopping briefly in Rome, then the Sudan, where it was at least 112 degrees in the shade. I thought, "Why did I want to come to Africa? Why did I want to go any place where it is 112 degrees in the shade?" Addis Ababa, though, is 7,000 feet above sea level, so it was cool and pleasant. When we arrived, it was Meskal Day, a Coptic Christian festival on September 27 celebrating the end of the rainy season and welcoming the spring. Meskal means "cross." The festival is about an ancient

Ethiopian queen said to have gone to Jerusalem and to have found the cross on which Christ was crucified. I saw a cross in Meskal Square, a huge open area, where a big bonfire was burning in a ring around the cross so evil wouldn't get to it: a cleansing symbol.

We were met at Haile Selassie International Airport by the mayor of Addis Ababa, who, it developed, was my traveling companion's husband. The area was gorgeous. The mountains were a deep green with a multitude of yellow daisylike flowers. The women wore long white dresses with beautifully embroidered floral trimming around the bottom. The dresses and embroidered shawls were of handwoven cotton, often of several sheer layers.

The mountains, the flowers, the beautiful clothes almost made me forget where I was. I had brought a camera but forgot to use it. Half a dozen of "my" students had come to the plane in gaily decorated cars with "Welcome Sister" signs on the sides. I was so happy to see them.

The boys drove me in style to the Ras (Duke) Hotel, a new building, very nice, on a hill. I had a large room with tall windows overlooking the city. The grounds were beautiful, all well manicured, with many flowers. It was three or four days, though, before I became acclimated to the high altitude. At first I thought there was something wrong with my heart, but I was advised just to take it easy and not run around the way I was used to doing. The boys led me on a round of parties, introducing me to their families and friends.

When I arrived the emperor was not in Addis Ababa but in one of the provinces. He had a palace in each of the thirteen provinces, something of a necessity as the roads were so poor that travel took a long time. When the emperor returned I was summoned to the palace for tea. Alle Felege Selam and Nerayo Assayus accompanied me. Alle had stopped by my hotel the day before to help me select my wardrobe. On meeting the emperor in Chicago I could wear what Chicagoans do, but in Ethiopia I should wear what the court prescribed. Sort of, "In Rome do as the Romans do."

I had a beautiful taffeta dress, blue and white with a little yellow, which I had bought at Saks Fifth Avenue in Chicago. Alle picked this one. About 10 A.M. on tea day I received a call from the palace to come immediately, as the emperor would be busy that afternoon. "I can't wear a taffeta dress in the morning," I lamented to Alle. "It won't matter, just wear it," he said.

Alle and Nerayo drove me to the midtown palace in their Volkswagen. The palace was an enormous mass with big iron gates, soldiers stiffly on guard. The soldiers saluted me as we drove through the gates, and I felt just like a celebrity. One of the soldiers had been in my home during his military training in the United States. He recognized me and smiled as he saluted. Inside I was escorted into an anteroom upstairs. Several men were waiting to see his majesty, apparently about to present their diplomatic credentials as representatives of their countries. They asked me what country I was representing. I said I wasn't representing any, that I wasn't a diplomat, just a tourist lucky enough to be the emperor's guest.

The boys had taught me to curtsy three times on meeting the emperor: once on entering the room and two more times as I approached. I had been practicing for days to make sure I would do it beautifully, but now I remember only that I curtsied once. The emperor was seated at his desk in a huge room. He seemed a block away as I entered. When I finally reached him he stood up, stretching his arms out to greet me, then motioning me to sit down opposite him. He welcomed me to Ethiopia in English, then spoke only in Amharic, with an interpreter translating what he said into English.

Haile Selassie had a way of relaxing people that was very helpful because of the time necessary to translate each bit of conversation. He asked questions about how I liked Ethiopia and apologized for not being in residence when I had arrived. The interpreter told me that, as the emperor's guest, I was to stay in the imperial compound. "No, no, tell him I don't want to," I replied. "I want to stay with my children and meet with their families. I'm quite comfortable where I am."

The emperor frowned. Probably it was the first time anyone had refused to stay in the palace! In my case, ignorance was bliss. But I think that by refusing to stay at the palace I cemented a friendship with the whole country, as I would never otherwise have had the opportunities to visit as I wanted, to see the people.

I visited four provinces on Ethiopian Airlines, in much smaller planes than that I had taken to Addis Ababa from Athens. I found that many people were poor, but they had plenty of food. Much produce was shipped to the huge market in Addis, where there were all kinds of luscious fruits and vegetables, herb seasonings and seeds. I particularly liked the oranges, much sweeter and juicier than the famous Jaffa oranges of Israel. They were so plentiful farmers would come by truck and dump loads of oranges on the street, with people helping themselves. In Harra the oranges were growing bigger than grapefruit. Many Ethiopians in Addis Ababa had their own gardens with citrus fruits and other edibles. They didn't seem to know what to do, though, with avocados, which they fed to the livestock. Watermelons also were not eaten much by the people. I saw collard greens, just as tender as could be, which grew like bushes. I think almost every vegetable I'd heard of was grown there. In 1955 there was no starvation.

During my three months in Ethiopia Haile Selassie celebrated his twenty-fifth year as emperor, the Lion of Judah. I was invited to many of the affairs. I also was given a Fiat and was in a parade, one of many during this celebration. I met the whole royal family: the crown prince, Asfa Wossen; the other princes and princesses; and Makonnen, the Duke of Harra, the emperor's second son. The duke and John Robinson had been very good friends back in the 1930s and '40s.

One night I was invited to the duke's house in the capital for dinner. (He also had a palace of his own in the province of Harra.) A chauffeured car was sent for me. The soldier guarding the house came out to meet me holding an enormous ornate umbrella with a gold fringe around the rim. "It isn't raining," I thought. But it was all protocol. The meal was served in many courses, with all kinds of meats and vegetables and fruits. The duke, his wife, one of the princes, and I seemed lost in the enormous dining room.

One of the jubilee celebrations was given at the palace, and I was invited. I went with David Talbot and his wife. He was from the

West Indies, editor of the *Ethiopian Herald,* and a friend of the boys. He also operated a secretarial school. This reception was the most elegant one I'd attended, with an imported orchestra playing some Western music and diplomats from all over the world. A guard came to David in the midst of a conversation to say the duke wanted me to come to the area where the royal family was seated. The duke stood up and said, "Sister"—everyone called me Sister, probably because the boys had told them—"I want you to meet the rest of the family." Everything was very quiet for a few moments, all attention focused on my meeting the royal family. I must say I enjoyed the attention.

Abuna Theophilus, archbishop of the Ethiopian Coptic Christian Church, also invited me to dinner one evening. I had met him in Chicago when he was touring the United States. Nerayo and Alle accompanied me. I counted seven courses. It was a good dinner, but I thought they would never stop serving. There was also much aged Ethiopian wine.

After that, U.S. Ambassador Joseph Simonson, who already knew about me because stories about my visit had appeared in the newspapers almost daily, stopped to talk. I was delighted when he invited me to the U.S. embassy for lunch. The boys said, "You don't have to go unless you want to," but Mulatu Debebe, who knew protocol, thought I should. The ambassador wanted to know the whole story of my background because he couldn't understand why there was such a fuss about my visit. Mulatu, who had accompanied me, said, "I would like to answer that question. She was our American mother while we were at school in the United States. She did everything for us, came to the schools to check on our progress, helped us get what we needed, kept us at her house, when the rest of the people didn't do anything. We were segregated. We will never be able to repay her for her thoughtfulness and love." I thought his concern for me was just lovely.

One of the consuls took me aside and complained that he had not been invited into any Ethiopian homes, as I had. I explained that, eventually, he would be invited "when they know you better."

The ambassador told me that *Life* magazine had been in Addis Ababa doing a story about Abuna Theophilus. He was very surprised to learn I'd had dinner with the archbishop, when he had not. How did insignificant Janet Harmon Bragg get invited to the homes of the greats of Ethiopia? I don't think he fully understood how much bias there still was against blacks in the United States at that time—any blacks, even children of high-ranking parents from foreign countries, diplomats, and the wealthy and well educated. The people in Ethiopia knew that I had helped their children do well in a difficult environment, and they were grateful.

After a few weeks in Addis Ababa I felt I belonged there. I had old friends, the young men whom I called "my boys," and I had met their families and been invited into their homes. I even came to feel that my ancestors might well have come from Ethiopia. My features and skin color were so similar, not at all like those of peoples from South and West Africa. If I'd been able to speak Amharic, I'm sure I could have passed for an Ethiopian.

After one of my trips to the provinces with Mulatu I felt even more as if Ethiopia were my ancestral homeland. We had flown to Lake Tana, source of the Blue Nile, to see an ancient fourteenth-century Coptic church and monastery. We didn't get into the monastery, as it is high up on a cliff, inaccessible except by rope ladder and forbidden to women. But at the church I had the eerie feeling that I had been there before. Somehow, even before we went inside, I knew what the interior looked like. The church was small and round, built of stone, brick, and wood, with windows like peepholes, so that it was fairly dark. After a while we got used to the dimness. Inside the Trinity was depicted in mosaic on the walls, along with saints and other biblical representations. It was so clean—but it never had been cleaned, I was told, which seemed marvelous. Women sat only in an outer circle, with men in the middle and the clergy at the very center. An ornate rope divided the three sections.

After we came out I saw bamboo growing by the lake, with a path between the high stalks. I started to walk down the path as if going home. Mulatu called to me, "Sister, where are you going?" and I replied, "I don't know, but I've been here before. Are there any *tukle* [huts] on the other end of this path?" He said, "Yes, people live there," and I knew I'd been there before. I'm not a believer in déjà vu or in reincarnation, but something had impelled me down that path as if I were going to a familiar place.

I wish I had been able to see those huts and the people living in them. Mulatu, though, stopped me because we had to return to the boat which would take us across the lake to our plane and back to Addis Ababa. The plane had seats along the side, with the passengers' chickens, sheep, goats, and produce in the center or under the benches. It was strange to see a modern conveyance like an airplane carrying live animals, particularly after coming directly from an ancient church and my "vision."

Days afterward that feeling about the church was still on my mind. But that night, at a party given for me by Seifu M. Selassie (no relation to the royal family), a little girl of about 12 came up to me and touched my hand and held it. "I want to go back to the States with you," she said. "Why?" I asked, and she replied, "I love you, and I want to get an education." She was Tseganet Makonnen, young sister of my first boy, Seifu Selleke. "Wouldn't you get lonesome?" I asked. Seifu came up and remarked, "You'll be an old lady by the time you finish school," to which she said, "I don't care if I'm 50 years old!" All I could say was "We'll talk about it." Several days later Seifu said that Tseganet still wanted to go. It was then that I learned that Ethiopian girls never were sent out of the country to be educated, as were the boys. I decided that if Tseganet really wanted to come, I would be delighted to help her, even though permission had to be obtained from the emperor himself. Seifu made arrangements for his little sister to fly to the United States, getting her a passport and a visa and making other necessary preparations. This process took so long that my own visa nearly had expired. It was time for me to get back to Sumner and our nursing homes.

I returned to the palace to bid farewell to his majesty and to thank him for the invitation and the all-expenses-paid tour. He was very pleased I had so enjoyed my sojourn in his country. He said, in perfect English, "I notice not many of your children are getting married." It was true. Although I had expected to come for a wedding, or to see "grandchildren," none of the boys was married.

"In talking with one of the boys," I said, "he told me he wanted an educated wife, so that when he came home he would have someone to talk with on an educated level." The boy had told me he could remember how, when he was a child, his mother would play with him, but when she heard his father's footsteps she immediately would get her shawl, sit in a corner, and insert eucalyptus leaves in her nostrils. He learned later that his mother pretended to be sick so she would have some security, but that was not what he wanted in a wife.

His majesty already had realized that his would be a better country if more women also were educated, but it was not until then that he provided scholarships for them to study in Europe and the United States. Tseganet would soon get her wish and join me in the States.

As I was about to leave, the emperor offered me a lion cub from his private zoo. He had a number of African species in the zoo, as well as the old lion I'd seen lying on some rear steps. I had to decline, thanking him but explaining that I could not possibly keep a lion in a Chicago nursing home.

That first trip to Ethiopia impressed me very much. It was inspiring to see that a country could be governed by blacks, and that blacks were those who made the country successful. I was anxious to travel more, to learn more. Eventually I traveled throughout East and West Africa and in Europe. My only regret was that Sumner didn't want to travel, but then I might not have been able to go abroad again if it hadn't been for his willingness to stay at home and look after our nursing-home business.

9

More Students and Travels

My travels were becoming something of a fairy tale. No
one would have believed that the kids I had befriended
in the States were now ambassadors who would
entertain me so royally.

Tseganet arrived two weeks after I returned home, with another girl,
Haregone Selassie, Seifu Selassie's sister. I met them in New York.
My friend Clifford Campbell, principal of the Dunbar High School,
took them in even though they had brought no school transcripts
with them. Both girls stayed with Sumner and me in our home.
Tseganet knew how little education Haregone had had and tutored
her to help her keep up. Tseganet was later relieved of this chore
when Haregone moved to Washington with her father.

After Tseganet had spent a year at Dunbar, I enrolled her in the
University of Chicago lab school, where she did very well. I also obtained
a tutor for her to assure that she continued to do so, as the other students
at the school were exceptionally talented. After graduation from high
school she earned a scholarship to study at a university in Simla, India.

A few years after Tseganet left for India, another Ethiopian girl, Zennebework Teshome, whom we called "Zannie" and whose name meant "raining gold," arrived and stayed with us for the summer before going to Southern Illinois University at Carbondale as a prepharmacy student. After graduation she went to the Illinois College of Pharmacy in Chicago, staying with us until her last year, when she lived in a dormitory. She graduated from both schools with high honors. We sponsored her at the Links Cotillion, put on by an outstanding nationwide charitable organization which does much for the black community. I made a fashionable dress of white peau de soie, with rhinestones embroidered all over the bodice. It was very beautiful.

Zannie met her future husband, Maurice Hebert, an American black, while in pharmacy school. After graduation she worked in a hospital pharmacy. She and Maurice wanted to get married, but her family in Ethiopia objected strongly because he was an American. Maurice followed her to Ethiopia when she went home for a visit, and asked her family for her hand in marriage. Zannie's family, on first meeting Maurice, couldn't believe he wasn't Ethiopian, as he looked so much like them.

They exacted a stipulation that Maurice and Zannie could marry if he learned to speak Amharic. Maurice replied that Zannie spoke English well. "I'm not marrying the family, I'm marrying her," he maintained. Disregarding her brothers' wishes, they went to the Addis Ababa city hall, were married, toured Europe for a honeymoon, and returned to the United States. Maurice, convinced that most health problems stemmed from poor eating habits, opened a health foods store with Zannie in Chicago, and both abandoned their former profession of pharmacy. Maurice, an amateur pilot, was later killed in a plane crash when their two children—a girl, Rachel, and a boy, Tshome—were still young. Today Zannie is a very successful businesswoman in Chicago.

Zewditu Haile came to me after my second visit to Ethiopia in 1965. I had met her while staying with Alle Felege Selam, one of my first boys. A relative, she took care of his children after his divorce. She was a dear little girl, very tiny, very ambitious and studious, and she wanted to come to the States for a better education. I sent her plane fare, and she lived with Sumner and me, attending Kennedy-King Junior College in Chicago.

Earlier I had met some of the nuns at Barat College of the Sacred Heart in Lake Forest when I was giving a program on Africa there. The college already had several African girls as students. A sister, whose name now escapes me, told me when I called her that she would investigate the possibility of a scholarship at Barat for Zewditu. She said the board would be meeting in a few days, and she would bring up the subject. Within a week she called back to say she had succeeded and that Zewditu would have a scholarship. I wanted Zewditu to study home economics, as there were so many things she needed to know about how to take care of herself. She was unhappy at first because she didn't want to leave me, but after I explained we were just thirty miles apart and the telephone was at hand, she came to like the college and her classmates. She was very happy within a few months. The nuns and other students were very kind to her.

While at Barat Zewditu met Muleneh Azene, an Ethiopian graduate student in engineering at Northwestern University. They were married at Barat in a traditional Ethiopian ceremony. Sadly, I couldn't attend, as Sumner was ill and we were at our winter home in Tucson, but I relived the occasion through color photos they sent me.

When Sumner and I later visited Zewditu at her home in Baton Rouge, where her husband was teaching engineering at Southern University, she told me she was so happy I had urged her to study home economics rather than pharmacy. Because of Zannie's and Maurice's success with pharmacy, she originally had thought she should follow in their footsteps. The Azenes lived in a large house with their three children and were happy and successful.

All of "my children" have generally done very well in their respective lives, and I'm grateful to have been able to be of help to them.

My travels abroad didn't end with my three-month sojourn in Ethiopia. Ten years later, in 1965, my friend VeNona Roberts Johnson, the Chicago high school principal who had canvassed the neighborhood to gain permission to open my nursing home on Kimbark Avenue, was asked to go to Sierra Leone in West Africa to instruct teachers there in some of the classroom procedures used in the United States. Her mother approved of the trip only if I accompanied her. It didn't take much persuasion for me to agree. As VeNona's expenses were to be paid by the government, I would have to defray my own expenses and make my own arrangements.

I had met Patricia Tucker Kabbah when she was a language student at the University of Chicago, and we had become very good friends. Knowing she now lived in the capital of Freetown, Sierra Leone, I wrote to her and asked her about accommodations in an African home, as I didn't want to live in a hotel. My chief objective in traveling was to meet the people. She cabled back that I would be welcome at her house. Happy about this, I then informed VeNona that I was ready to go with her to Sierra Leone.

Along with twenty other teachers, we set out on Pan American from New York to Dakar, Senegal. Although the flight was long, we had a wonderful time on the plane. The place I remember most clearly in Dakar was the old slave market, with its auction block. As I stood there, in my mind's eye I could see those poor black souls chained together, poor human beings treated worse than cattle. I could imagine them being dragged into the holds of dark, dirty, dingy ships, too many of them dying as they were transported to the New World. And here I was, many years later, flying higher in the sky than they had been down in the bottom of the ships.

We have to stop and think about these things. Maybe those slaves were praying to God, just as we do. Maybe they asked the question, "Why me, God?" Sometimes I become really bitter. We all should take time to smell the roses; we all should have the *opportunity* to smell the roses. I also thought about the blacks who sold their brethren to the slave traders. Did they really make enough, in money or goods, to make such traitorous acts worthwhile? Were they ashamed afterward? To me, they were worse than the white slave traders.

Then it was on to Sierra Leone, our destination. Pat, a petite young lady, met me at the airport with a chauffeur-driven limousine and drove me to her huge modern home overlooking the Atlantic Ocean. On the grounds she had all kinds of fruit trees, as well as a vegetable garden. And she had a gardener, a cook, and other servants. I learned that Pat served as secretary-interpreter for the prime minister of Sierra Leone and was a very important person in her own right. I recalled how she had struggled to get through the University of Chicago, a sacrifice that led to her success in her homeland. Accommodations for VeNona and the other teachers were extremely poor in comparison with the luxury in which I found myself.

Pat had planned many activities and parties for me, so that I could meet her friends and learn about her country. One of her friends invited me to a dinner at which she served *foo-foo,* made from a turnip-like root; it takes two days to prepare. I was embarrassed, but I just couldn't eat it. Its consistency was something like tapioca, but gooey. I apologized and said, "This is something I will have to cultivate a taste for." Nevertheless, I was eager to try other native foods.

At one point I asked Pat if I could invite VeNona to dinner, and she replied in her musical English, "Of course, Madame, we'd be very happy to have her." A lovely dinner was prepared, a mixture of international and native foods. A butler served us in grand style. At the beginning of the meal there was very little conversation. Neither Pat nor her husband, Tejan, an Oxford graduate who was an attorney with the government, a high position, said much of anything. Finally I asked why no one was talking, learning that they were self-conscious because they thought VeNona, who is very light-skinned, was not black. I told them she *was* black, and the conversation took off, running from one thing to another. We talked and talked until the wee hours of the morning.

While VeNona was still at work in Sierra Leone, I traveled to Liberia. I had hoped to go by boat from Freetown but could not book passage, so I flew to Monrovia, the capital. From there I took a cab to Kakata, about fifty miles into the bush, where my friend Ellen Moore Hopkins lived with her husband. Ellen was an African nurse whom I'd met when she was in the United States raising funds for her project, an orphanage and maternal welfare clinic. She had graduated from Sarah Lawrence College in midwifery. Instead of surprising her, however, I was the one to be surprised, for I found she was away, traveling in the United States again to raise funds. Her husband, Richard, a bishop of his church, insisted that I stay in their home. He tried to make it very comfortable for me, despite the fact that some of the goings-on seemed rather grotesque.

That evening two of the clinic's little orphan girls came into the living room where we were sitting and talking. They carried towels and a basin of water, and proceeded to wash Richard's feet. One little girl took off a sandal and put his foot in the basin, manipulating his toes and washing his dirty foot. The other girl did the same with the other foot. Then they rubbed down his feet with alcohol and oil. I was dumbfounded and hurt, seeing those little girls washing his great big ugly old feet. I asked, "What are they doing this for?" thinking it was some kind of ritual. He replied. "This is one of their chores. They do this every night."

When I got back to Chicago I talked about this experience and how poorly cared for the children were. The Chicago Graduate Nurses Association, with Frankie Thompson and her husband, Charles, a pharmacist, had set up a fund to send money, physician's samples of antibiotics, and vitamins to Ellen's clinic and orphanage. The group had sent mattresses, and Sumner and I had sent a refrigerator, which Sears delivered.

Ellen heard about my report and wrote to me, saying how unhappy she was about it. I didn't want to be too critical, but it seemed to me that the refrigerator should have been used for the children, not for the bishop and his wife, and that the money, too, should have been spent on the children and not on a huge chapel. Food for the children—mostly rice and a few vegetables—was cooked in big pots out-of-doors. One of the girls, about 14 years old, told me that some of the things we had sent were being eaten by rats in the storage room.

The night I visited, Richard told me that the little girl who would stay with me (because I didn't want to stay alone with him) had been punished for stealing. She had been stripped nude and forced to stand on a table in front of the other orphans. I asked why he would embarrass her so, and he said, "It will teach her a lesson not to steal again." I asked how he could be so sure she would not steal again. It was all too much for me.

On the third day Bishop Hopkins said he had to go into Monrovia to see his doctor, as he had "worms." I went with him to town, where I met the doctor and his wife, an American nurse. She asked me, "Do you like it out there?" and I replied, "Ellen isn't there, and it makes a difference, as I don't know her husband."

"You don't have to stay. You can come back here," she suggested. She told me where the Ethiopian embassy was—not far away, within walking distance from the office. Despite the heat—the sun was blazing down—I walked to the embassy and into a delightfully cool anteroom. I told the receptionist I wanted a visa for Ethiopia, but she explained that the embassy secretary was not in. Because of the heat and my experiences during the past two days, I told her I would wait.

I asked the receptionist who the ambassador was and she told me he was Haile Marian. What luck! Haile had been one of "my" children. During my wait the secretary returned, and I found he was the brother of another of "my" children. Then the ambassador came downstairs and saw me.

"Sister, what are you doing here?" he shouted. "I'm looking for my tribe," I joked, and he said, "You know where your tribe is."

Haile asked me where I was staying and offered accommodations at the embassy. "You must come here," he said. He didn't have to offer twice. He even drove me out to Kakata to pick up my luggage.

I was a happy soul at the embassy, where I met Haile's wife and children. We talked of old times in Chicago. Mrs. Marian wore a belt with many keys. I asked her the purpose of the keys, and she explained that everything had to be locked up, as the native help would "liberate" anything not nailed down.

During the next two days the ambassador and his wife made it very, very pleasant for me. They did everything possible to make me comfortable. At one point Haile asked, "Guess who is in Ghana?" and then related that Ephraim, another of "my" boys, was Ethiopian ambassador to Ghana. I could say little more than "You're kidding!" I'd had no intention, originally, of going to Liberia, let alone Ghana. Haile called Ephraim on the telephone and told him to expect me. The next day I flew to the capital, Accra. Ephraim sent an assistant, who drove up in a limousine with the Ethiopian flags on standards at the front. At the embassy Ephraim apologized for not meeting me, as he had been at a conference. He asked how long I would stay, hoping we could have a long visit between his duties.

"I want to see something of Ghana; a few days," I said. Ephraim told me he would have a dinner party the next night at the swanky Ivory Coast Hotel, inviting other diplomats to meet me. I was being treated royally.

At the party I was surprised to note that so many of the wives were white and blonde, not African women. Ephraim explained that the men had married while they were in school or while working in European countries, where there was no color barrier such as found in the United States.

Then Ephraim asked, "Guess who is in Lagos, Nigeria?" Seifu Selleke, the very first of "my" boys, was there with the World Health Organization. So after a few days in Accra, off I went to Lagos! Ephraim had called Seifu to alert him that "a friend" of his was coming, but he didn't tell him it was me. Seifu was at the airport with his wife and child, waiting for who-knew-what to get off the plane. When he saw me, the last to disembark, he didn't know what to do with the baby—give him to his wife, or hug me with the child between us. That hug was so fierce the baby cried. We had a great reunion.

I was taken around Lagos and met Seifu's friends. I met the Ethiopian ambassador to Nigeria, David Devit, who also made my

stay pleasant. Pat, from Sierra Leone, had given me a letter of introduction to a man in Lagos, although I hadn't known at the time
whether I would go to Nigeria. Seifu was very impressed as, he said,
this man in Lagos was one of the most influential people in the
country. We went to the man's office and found he was a very
down-to-earth person who wanted to know what he could do for
us. We explained how Seifu came to be my "son." Seifu told the
man—you'd think I could remember his name, as he was so important in the country, but I can't—he needed a larger house for his
family, so this man obtained one and later Seifu's family moved in.
Unfortunately, it was so large and expensive that Seifu couldn't
afford to keep it up on his World Health Organization salary.

VeNona met me in Lagos, and then we flew across the continent
to Ethiopia, my second visit. She was reintroduced to "my" children,
who made it very pleasant for her.

My travels were becoming something of a fairy tale. No one
would have believed that the kids I had befriended in the States were
now ambassadors who would entertain me so royally. Little things
you do for people can be big things for others. What I had done had
touched the lives of these boys, motivated them to succeed. My small
efforts were being returned a hundredfold. I never felt a stranger in
traveling, even in Europe, because there was always someone to meet
me, someone who had been in my home and had been helped in
some small way to get an education. No one could have had those
efforts appreciated so much as mine were.

Later, in Addis Ababa, after VeNona's mission had ended, we met
again and stayed at the Ethiopian Hilton Hotel. For a week we
visited all of "my family" in the capital. Tseganet, now married to
Arthur Blumeris, was there, along with their son Michael, who was
about two. Anna Koldheimen, a Chicago school principal and
teacher on a mission to Ethiopia, joined us on our rounds.

VeNona, Anna, and I then flew to Cairo, spending several days
viewing the pyramids and the Sphinx across the river in the biblical
Land of Goshen. VeNona and I climbed inside one of the pyramids

until it got so hot and the air so bad I decided we should return. "What took you so long?" asked VeNona, and we burst out laughing. We went back, up the down staircase, the way we had come, only to have someone say we were not supposed to be going back. "Just watch us," VeNona said. We, and those on the way down, kept saying, "Excuse me, excuse me," until we were outside.

From Cairo we flew to Rome on Japan Airlines, which lost our luggage. We had planned to go to the opera, and we went anyway, despite the necessity for wearing our traveling suits. That night we used bath towels for nightgowns. The next day the airline agent told us to go shopping at the airline's expense, as the luggage hadn't turned up. We finished buying most of the clothing and other necessities just as our bags arrived. We were told to keep on shopping, as we had been so nice about the lost bags, and so we did, buying some very fashionable Italian knits.

After two months away it was time to return to my hardworking husband, Sumner, who still insisted he didn't want to travel. The next two years I stayed at home. In mid-1972 I went once more to Ethiopia, returning again the following year as a "travel consultant." By then I'd completed a travel agency course and gotten a job with Arrington's Travel Agency on North Michigan Avenue. Mike Arrington and I were in the same class, and when he opened the agency he gave me a job as a travel consultant. I'd had enough experience traveling on the "Dark Continent" to escort a group of fifteen black senior citizens, all first-class throughout. I was anxious to do extremely well on this trip, as it would mean I could continue as a travel consultant, with my commission paying my way abroad. (I had been named honorary consul general for Ethiopia in Chicago, at no pay, and could provide visas. Eventually that became too expensive, particularly as I had to meet and greet visiting diplomats, and I gave it up.)

Some of the women on my 1972 tour had been abroad previously, but none had traveled in Africa. I don't think they had ever experienced, or even expected, the royal treatment they found on this trip.

We flew on TWA from New York to Rome to Nairobi, Kenya, where we went on safari for five days, living in tents. We drove out on the Masai Mara in a Land Rover equipped so we could stand up and shoot pictures. At one point we saw a lioness leap on a zebra, clamp her teeth around its mouth, then strangle it, disembowel it, and drive off hyenas before her mate returned to help her drag the carcass to their den. It was fascinating to watch her as she prepared the zebra for her family. The female lion is the only one to hunt for the family; the male waits for her to "bring home the bacon." Everyone was fatigued by the pace we set, except for one woman who was 80 years old.

Our next stop was to have been Uganda, where I had been earlier, but we were warned to go only at our own risk, as Idi Amin was expelling all Asians and we didn't know what else he might do. In Nairobi I tried to book us into Addis Ababa, but the travel agent said that was impossible. Naturally, I said we would be welcome. We both raised our voices. Then a man walked in whom I recognized as an Ethiopian. I said "hello" in Amharic and told him of the difficulties we were having. He turned out to be the public relations representative for the Ethiopian Hilton in Addis Ababa, where I had stayed previously. Our problems were solved. He directed me to the Ethiopian Airlines office down the street, where he made our reservations for the next day. Thus, we had two extra days in Ethiopia and time for my tourists to meet "my kids" and visit in their homes. Tourists seldom have an opportunity to meet with the peoples in the countries they visit, so this was an unusual opportunity for my ladies. They were so happy, particularly as the Ethiopians were celebrating Meskal, their spring festival.

We went on to Axum, home of the legendary Queen of Sheba, to Gondar, home of the Falashas (black Jews), and to Asmara in Eritrea near the Red Sea, places few American tourists had ever seen. On the way back we stayed in Rome for two days and did some shopping. We were away three weeks and had a marvelous time, though everyone was glad to get home.

This trip was so successful I could have led others, but I was so worn out that instead I just booked several trips and did not go. In

1974 I went to Europe, with Sumner again staying home. I visited Sweden, Norway, Finland, and Denmark, as well as Germany and Italy. Cleo Scott, who had been with me on the African tour, planned this trip. Another friend, Beatrice King, decided she also wanted to go. Her passport had expired, and we had to wait ten days before she could get a new one and the necessary visas, which took some of the time we would have spent on the trip. Nevertheless, we had a fine time.

In Stockholm, our first stop, one of "my children," Tedelee Kibrat, met us at the airport. He had prepared only for two of us, but managed. He had bought a new Volvo station wagon, and he and his daughter, Mimi, drove us around the country and all the way down to Rome. We took the ferry to Denmark, where we visited Copenhagen, then drove down through West Germany and Austria to Italy and Rome. On the return we had hoped to go to several Balkan countries, but Bea had neglected to get her visas, so we drove to Dresden and Leipzig in East Germany, and from there back to Sweden.

In Leipzig the hotel wouldn't accept Bea's passport, claiming there was something wrong with it, but Tedelee, who spoke excellent German, as well as the languages of all the other countries we visited, told the clerk he had "three old American ladies on my hands, and they might die if they can't have a place to stay." That worked, and we were able to spend the night there. Because there were three of us "oldsters" and the hotel had only two twin-bed rooms, Tedelee managed to get me a roll-away bed. Luckily, I had to sleep on it only one night.

On our return to Sweden Tedelee had to go back to his work as a civil engineer, so we went to Norway and Finland by rail on our Eurailpasses, on our own. I had hoped to fly to Leningrad from Helsinki, but again Bea had no visa, so we couldn't go. We flew back to Stockholm and home to Tucson. Except for several trips to Mexico and one to Singapore, that was my last time abroad. Somehow one thing had just led to another until I had traveled extensively in Africa and Europe. It all was an excellent education, as—besides seeing the glories of these countries—I was able to meet the people.

10

New Honors

I expect to pass through this world but once; any good
therefore that I can do, or any kindness that I can show
to any fellow creature, let me do it now; let me not
defer or neglect it, for I shall not pass this way again.

Attributed to Stephen Grellet (1773–1855)

That quotation has meant a great deal to me. Despite the bias I
encountered both in my vocation and avocations, because I was a
woman and black, I think I've led a charmed life. Often it was difficult, but I enjoyed every minute.

While I was proud of what I had accomplished, I was unaware that
anyone else knew about it or cared, or that I was to become a part of
aviation history. In the late 1970s I met Rufus Hunt, a black Federal
Aviation Administration (FAA) employee at the Chicago Air Route
Traffic Control Center, at a meeting of the Tuskegee Airmen Dodo
chapter in Chicago. He told me that the FAA's Great Lakes region
public affairs office was looking for photos of Chicago's black aviation pioneers for a display they were putting together. Rufus took
me to regional headquarters, and I became fascinated with what the

staff was doing. When they asked me to help I was most happy to do so. The photos showed our early days at Robbins and Harlem airports and illustrated some of the struggles we endured.

The display was exhibited in Chicago at the Carter G. Woodson Library, named for the prominent black educator who originated Negro History Week, which eventually developed into Black History Month, now celebrated nationwide during February. Although that library contains the city's black history collection, at the time it had absolutely nothing on blacks in aviation, despite the fact that Chicago was the home of black aviation. At the end of the exhibit the library was presented with copies of the photos for its archives. The display was also exhibited at Chicago's main public library and several branches before moving on to Howard University and the Smithsonian Institution's National Air and Space Museum (NASM) in Washington, D.C.

The FAA and the National Air and Space Administration (NASA) later invited me to Howard University for a three-day symposium at which educators from all over the country were shown black accomplishments and urged to use these achievements in their classrooms. Earlier, the FAA exhibit had been shown during a convention of Negro Airmen International at NASM. The display was seen by NASM's Donald Lopez, who had been thinking of a black exhibit ever since a white museum patron had asked why there were no blacks depicted among America's aviation pioneers at the museum.

As part of the Howard conference, a program was held at NASM at which I spoke, along with "Chief" Anderson, the famed Tuskegee flight instructor who had helped me years before, and Lt. Gen. Benjamin O. Davis Jr., USAF (ret.), the first black general in the U.S. Air Force. My legs still wobble when I think of that speech I made in the big IMAX theater, but it was only the first of several. An elegant reception followed.

Finally NASM realized it should recognize black achievements in aviation and aerospace. Dr. Von Hardesty was assigned as the curator for the task of developing an exhibit; he was joined later by

Dominick Pisano. The result was "Black Wings: The American Black in Aviation," an exhibit that opened in September 1982.

The FAA public affairs office in Chicago and I were among the first whom Dr. Hardesty interviewed for "Black Wings," which tells the relatively unknown story of the black experience in aviation from the days of early flight to today's space shuttles. I was in six of the pictures. For the grand opening in Washington I received a handsome invitation from the secretary of the Smithsonian and NASM's acting director to attend the "Black Wings" premiere with all expenses paid.

The reception following the opening was fabulous. Visualize this! In the background was suspended a large model of a P-51 flown during the war by the all-black 332d Fighter Group of the U.S. Army Air Corps. There were planes everywhere. Government officials, including those of the FAA, were there to greet the black pioneers. Black commercial airline pilots, those from the Navy and the Air Force, and astronauts were there. Climaxing the brilliant evening was the announcement that a black astronaut, Lt. Col. Guion S. Bluford Jr., Ph.D., would be going up in space. Harold Hurd, Clyde Hampton, and Lt. Col. William Thompson, USAF (ret.), all from our Chicago group, also attended.

In the midst of all this glamour, the brilliant setting against which our exploits were at last revealed, nostalgia overwhelmed me and I fought back tears of joy as I reflected on the long road it had been to this: from the old Eagle Rock, which had been flown across the country by two blacks, to the space shuttle. The tragedy and frustration of that long road had been overcome by dogged determination, dedication, and a vision.

"Black Wings" toured the country, and I was asked to speak at many of the openings, including at the Franklin Institute in Philadelphia and at Chicago's Museum of Science and Industry during the 1985 Black Heritage Week. FAA civil rights directors, both in Chicago and Washington, awarded me certificates of achievement.

Our Chicago pioneers were invited to the 1984 opening of "Black Wings" at the Experimental Aircraft Association's new Air

Adventure Museum in Oshkosh, Wisconsin, during the association's fly-in, which annually attracts nearly a million visitors. There FAA Administrator Donald Engen presented me, Harold Hurd, "Chief" Anderson, Cornelius Coffey, and some others from our Chicago group with a most gratifying award, in leather cases lined with watered silk, signed by Great Lakes Region Director Paul K. Bohr. In part it cited me "for personal contributions to the development of the Black Wings Exhibit—which displays the special and historic role fulfilled by blacks in the development of American aviation—and for dedicated assistance in advancing aviation in the Great Lakes region." And if that weren't enough, *Smithsonian World,* the Institution's film program, interviewed me during the opening day at Oshkosh and the program later appeared on PBS television stations across the country. It was an exciting day, and I got a taste of being a celebrity.

I later was asked to speak at a "Black Wings" opening in Dover, Delaware, but I couldn't get there because of a blizzard. The last opening I attended was at the art museum in Phoenix in 1990. Three copies of the exhibit continued touring major cities and smaller communities around the country for several years.

In addition to the "Black Wings" tours, I have been honored to speak at FAA events and Black History Month celebrations at Davis-Monthan Air Force Base in Arizona and other military facilities. I also have spoken at school career-day events at Tucson public schools and at the Old Pueblo International Communications Club.

With this upsurge in interest in black aviation history, Dr. Von Hardesty, who put together the "Black Wings" exhibit, along with Dominick Pisano, also wrote a booklet with the same name as the exhibit, distributed by the Smithsonian Institution Press, with photos of me and others of our Chicago group. Harold Hurd's photo is on the cover.

In August 1984 Leon Watkins, FAA's director of civil rights, presented me with a certificate of appreciation, honoring me as "pioneer black female aviator and aircraft owner, charter member of the National Airmen's Association in America, in recognition of her role in establishing a place for black people in American aviation." The certificate, with FAA's gold and green emblem in color, is mounted on a beautiful walnut plaque. FAA's Great Lakes region public affairs office also engineered naming an intersection in my honor on the approach to Chicago O'Hare International Airport. Vector 228 is now called "Aunty," a name often used by young people who knew me. (Unfortunately, the five-letter designations already included "Janet" and "Bragg," while "Harmon" was more than five letters.)

In 1985 I was invited to Kennedy International Airport to receive the 14th Annual Bishop Wright Air Industry Award. I had been nominated by Ida Van Smith, herself a previous recipient of the award. I had heard about Ida Van long before I had the opportunity to meet her in 1982 at a Tuskegee Airmen convention in St. Louis, where we spent some time talking about our interest in aviation. She had been teaching school in Jamaica, New York, and working after class to get her Ph.D. in education. While sitting at her desk one day working on her dissertation, she became weary and tired. All of a sudden she decided to go out to the airport and learn where she could get flying lessons. Ida Van had wanted to fly all of her life. She was determined, as I had been much earlier. She knew what she wanted. She met the instructor and had a lesson that afternoon.

When school was out that year, she went to her hometown in the Carolinas and spent the whole summer learning to fly. She involved people from 8 to 80 in aviation education and, through her Ida Van Smith Flight Clubs, helped some young people attain their pilot certificates as a starting point for their aviation careers. Now she is a retired teacher in New York and an outstanding pilot who operates a flying program for young people on Long Island. We stay in touch via letter and telephone.

On the day Ida Van picked me up at the airport to go to the awards luncheon, I leaned over and whispered to her, "Who is Bishop Wright?" She explained that the award was named for the father of the Wright brothers, a bishop in the Episcopal church. I felt embarrassed not knowing who Bishop Wright was.

The award, sponsored by the Protestant Ecumenical Council at the airport, is presented annually to someone outstanding in aviation. I was proud to be honored, as Sen. Barry Goldwater from my retirement state of Arizona, Gen. "Chappie" James, and astronaut Neil Armstrong had been among the outstanding citizens honored earlier.

In Tucson in 1981, Dr. Charles "Chuck" Ford, principal of a local school and the first black city councilman, presented me with an award, incised on a sheet of Arizona copper, reading, "In recognition of your outstanding contributions to the City of Tucson in your many endeavors, I, on behalf of all citizens of this community, am pleased to bestow upon you the title of Outstanding Citizen of Tucson, the Sunshine City." Dr. Ford and his wife, Dr. Doris Ford, have been an inspiration to me. I am very proud of both of them. Sumner often said, "If I had a son like Chuck. . . ." In 1986 I received an award from the University of Arizona's black alumni and a beautiful thank-you note from the university president.

In 1989 I was invited to return to the National Air and Space Museum again, this time to participate in an audiovisual program, an oral history on videotape directed by my long-time friend Theodore W. "Ted" Robinson. Ted, a NASM visiting historian on leave from FAA's Eastern region, where he was a Flight Standards District Office supervisor, interviewed me for most of a day. The tapes, which include interviews with "Chief" Anderson, Dr. Lewis Jackson, and Cornelius Coffey, are available for scholars studying the achievements in aviation of black Americans.

I am very proud of the recognition given me by the National Air and Space Museum as well as of all the awards and the attention paid to me as an aviation pioneer. I don't think it has gone to my head, but sometimes I'm saddened that so many of us are dead or too ill to respond to the new deluge of invitations.

11

Reflections

According to recognized aerotechnical principles, the
bumblebee cannot fly, because of the shape and weight
of its body in relation to its total wing area. But the
bumblebee doesn't know this, so it goes ahead and flies
anyway! Surely our bodies were not designed to fly, but
our brains were, and we flew, too.

From barnstorming to the space shuttle, the story of black contributions to aviation has been packed with dramatic moments, and cannot be told without recognition of the role played by our black
women flyers. In the forefront, as the first to become a pilot, was the
immortal Bessie Coleman, who learned to fly in the early 1920s in
France because no one would teach a black woman in the United
States. In 1921 she obtained the first Fédération Aéronautique
Internationale (FAI) pilot's license awarded to a black woman. There
was no U.S. licensing then, and the FAI provided the only ones.
Black women such as Willa Brown of Chicago cofounded flying
schools, and neophyte women flyers dared, along with men, to fly
cracker-box early planes. These women were in the forefront, chal-
lenging racial barriers to their advancement in the field of aviation.

I am proud to have been a part of those pioneer days and am deeply appreciative of the honors and recognition extended to me as a role model for aspiring young black flyers today. The historic flight of the Wright brothers in 1903 captured the imagination of the American public only after a lapse of several years. Participation by black Americans in this new field did not come easily, owing to a widely held notion in the aviation community that blacks lacked the aptitude to fly. Blacks found themselves arbitrarily excluded from flight instruction, just as they were excluded from many other mainstream activities.

According to recognized aerotechnical principles, the bumblebee cannot fly, because of the shape and weight of its body in relation to its total wing area. But the bumblebee doesn't know this, so it goes ahead and flies anyway! Surely our bodies were not designed to fly, but our brains were, and we flew, too. I use this example at many of the events at which I am asked to speak.

As I take a retrospective view of those early days, I now realize that they provided me with more than the skills of flying. They provided me with skills in human relations and helped me to serve a twofold purpose: to convey both the price that had to be paid in laying the foundation for today, but, more important, to develop the kind of strength of character, the kind of determination necessary for setting a goal and allowing nothing to deter one from achieving that goal. All of these qualities are still needed today, by *all* young people if we expect our youth to build walls on the foundation laid through supreme sacrifice.

The importance of aviation to me personally, to all of us individually, and to our economy is something I try to explain in talks to schoolchildren. I don't think they really *can* understand what it was like in the 1930s when I learned to fly, because life today is so different. Those kids, if they have the will to do something and study hard to reach those goals, will get what they want, but it will be far easier than it was for me and those of my generation. In my talks I try to make the hard times amusing, so they will remember what I say and, eventually, understand to some degree what it was like back then.

Today one is held back only by the limits of one's own capabilities and not by man-made blocks and strings. Many opportunities exist for young minorities today, one of which is in the field of aeronautics. Our youth must be encouraged to prepare for and take advantage of those opportunities. Though my pilot's license no longer is current, so that I don't fly myself, I try to encourage young people to fly by working with schools in Tucson and with the Pima Air and Space Museum. There is so much that minority students can learn from aviation, even if they never fly themselves. I try to tell parents that their children should begin math and science courses as early as possible. The world is advancing so rapidly. I collect outdated aeronautical charts that show the practical uses of math. And aviation isn't just flying, it includes all the other services, such as flight attendants.

And, though my passport has expired, I always am ready to prove that this bumblebee can fly!

I went to Alabama in 1987 to attend the Negro Airmen International convention and fly-in at Tuskegee University. It was good to see old friends at Tuskegee and reminisce with "Chief" Anderson, the famed Tuskegee flight instructor, and his wife, Gertrude, who had invited me to be their houseguest. It all brought back memories. I was to fly with "Chief," but his plane developed hydraulic problems and we were grounded. I was very much impressed by the number of pilots and planes—some 75 planes from all four corners of the nation. The fly-in program included balloon busting, cross-country events, spot landings, and "bomb dropping."

I was pleased to find that the original Tuskegee airport buildings, used by the black pilots training for the Army during World War II, were still there, though I was appalled by their condition. I talked with some of the pilots at the convention, many of them sons and daughters of the Army Air Corps cadets of World War II and all of them obviously sufficiently well off to fly to the airport, about restoring the buildings. There are enough blacks in the United States to make contributions to do the work ourselves, possibly with aid from the National Trust for Historic Preservation. While the buildings probably no longer could be used for their original purpose, they would make a fine museum on black accomplishments in aviation. In the modern $9-million Gen. Daniel "Chappie" James Jr. aerospace class building on campus, one room is devoted to "Chief" Anderson's career. As a flight instructor he taught hundreds of young black cadets to fly and become good pilots. On a wall are displayed the awards, medals, and history of General James, the first black four-star USAF general. This is a good beginning, but the old buildings themselves are historic and should be preserved.

In 1989 I was invited to speak at Indiana University, but I was unable to complete my speech because I had a heart attack and ended up in the hospital. Later I was asked to be a guest at the inauguration of Dr. Johnnetta B. Cole, the first black to be president of my alma mater, Spelman College, since its founding in 1881. As part of the celebration various people gave talks on career possibilities for student graduates. My topic was on careers for black women in science, technology, and aviation.

In the years since I had been on the campus, there were many, many changes. Spelman is now a liberal arts college, primarily for black women. The presidential inauguration was highlighted by the presence of actor Bill Cosby, who announced a pledge of $20 million to the college. Most of the audience didn't realize that Cosby (whose wife, Camille, graduated from Spelman) actually had said "million." When it sunk in, everyone stood and applauded. In his speech he said he and Camille wanted to share some of their wealth. I was very much impressed by his saying we should all support our colleges. He mentioned that we often spend too much on shoes, knowing they would hurt our feet and then leaving them on a chair. Or we buy a dress, knowing it would be too small and hoping to lose some weight to wear it, but never losing any. We buy many things we actually don't need. We all should help the college of our choice, either directly or through the United Negro College Fund, he said.

His statements reminded me of instances when I thought I would like to buy something expensive, something I didn't really need—

like a new Jaguar or, if I weren't too old, another airplane. Why buy a Jaguar or an airplane with a limited life span, when I could provide a scholarship that would last for years? His speech encouraged me to give, and I hope it did the same for others in the audience. An investment in a human life continues on and on.

On my return to Tucson from the earlier symposium at Howard University, I wrote to the Federal Aviation Administration (FAA) in Washington (where there was a concerted effort at the time to promote aviation in schools), requesting stacks of literature. Then I talked with school principals, at least seven of them, about using the material in classes. Four of them approved of the program but did nothing to get it under way. The only one really interested was Dr. Chuck Ford, who had presented me with the "Outstanding Citizen of Tucson" award in 1981 and was one of Sumner's fraternity brothers. His school was not the type I was seeking, as its students came from more affluent neighborhoods and I wanted to reach less advantaged children. I was not successful then, but I haven't given up. The FAA hasn't given up either, though it no longer publishes the courses and other material for teachers and students.

Now I am working with the Adopt-a-School program at Pima Community College in Tucson, initiated by Dr. Johnny Bowens. To me the program is very interesting because it motivates children to accomplish more in school. After seeing a *60 Minutes* segment in which a New York philanthropist offered college scholarships to inner-city high school students who stayed in school and graduated with decent grades, Johnny was motivated to start his program with the sixth grade, selecting students who would work toward college. My club, the Ex-Chicagoans, sponsored a bridge tournament, raising enough money from the tournament and a program with paid ads for two scholarships. We are waiting anxiously to see what becomes of the students selected to receive our scholarships, and we also are looking forward to other projects that will help raise scholarship money.

As for "my children," many of the boys were slain or, like Haile Selassie, died in prison after the 1974 communist coup which ended the Lion of Judah's dynasty. I'm ever so grateful for the pleasure they gave me while visiting my home in Chicago and while I visited their homes during my travels in Africa and Europe. The current government in Ethiopia could use some of their expertise. If they did there wouldn't be so much poverty and such enormous inflation. I miss the boys, but I am thankful I could provide them with some assistance while they were studying in the United States. It was most rewarding to see them as ambassadors and in other important roles in Africa.

The three girls whom I sponsored and to whom I gave scholarships still write to me and call me on the telephone. We meet whenever we can, which is too seldom. They send me photos of their families, which I add to my scrapbooks. When Tseganet's husband, Arthur, died in Zimbabwe where he was a diplomat, I was one of the first she called, long distance, to give me the sad news. Fortunately, she has been able to support her daughter, Iris, who stayed with her when they came to New York, and her tall, handsome son, Michael. Tseganet sent Michael to me in Tucson while he attended Pima Community College and the University of Arizona, where he studied business administration.

My nursing career ended—officially—in 1972 when we closed the nursing homes on moving our winter home to Tucson. However, the talents and knowledge accumulated over the years of work and study always will be useful. Sumner, who died in 1986 after a long illness, benefited from that knowledge.

After Sumner died I terminated the lease on our Chicago apartment and moved everything to Tucson. Once I had everything together in one place, I could sift out the things I wanted to keep. Among the items I parted with was my fabulous leopard fur coat. I was reminded of the early morning call, at 4 or 5 A.M., in the late 1960s when Seifu phoned me. The first thing that comes to mind at such an hour is bad news—a death, accident, or something else terrible has happened. Not in this case, though.

"Hello, hello, is this Sister speaking?" a man's voice asked. "Yes, Sister, this is Seifu Selleke from Ethiopia. I'm coming to America next month. What do you want me to bring you?" Though still half asleep, I was happy to hear his voice. My joking reply was, "Bring me a leopard coat." He said, "I will try."

Well, when Seifu arrived in Chicago about three weeks later, he did bring me a full leopard coat designed by the furriers who also designed similar coats for Elizabeth Taylor and Jacqueline Onassis. And not only did he bring me a coat, but also a black leopard stole, which is very rare. I modeled the coat and stole in many charity fashion shows, enjoying the attention very much. By the time I closed the Chicago apartment, I found the coat was like paper, too old and fragile to keep. I still have the black leopard, though.

Despite the unforgotten drawbacks, some of them unforgivable, life generally has been very good to me. I hope that, by remembering the Golden Rule and the quotation at the beginning of the previous chapter, I have done as much for others as others have done for me.

Appendix

Friends and Colleagues Remember Janet Harmon Bragg

Harold Hurd

A major step was taken by people of color toward entering the field of aviation in 1933. That was the year we met Janet Harmon Waterford, as she was known then. John C. Robinson and Cornelius Coffey already were graduates of a flying school. Four other youths, including William Jackson and me, had begun building our own airplane in 1929, planning to teach ourselves to fly it. This project began to draw public attention and resulted in a surprise visit by Robinson and Coffey. They advised that they were attempting to organize an all-black class to attend the Curtiss Wright Flying School.

Jackson and I were delighted to hear of such plans, and we joined in the recruitment of a class of approximately 25 colored males and one female: Janet. Unbelievable! A girl interested in mechanics, airplanes, and flying? Beautiful, bronze, unassuming, and a nurse, Janet was truly interested in all aspects of aviation. Of course we had heard of Bessie Coleman, the first black aviatrix, who had received her pilot's license in France, but we knew nothing more about her flying experience.

During our first official meeting as a class we became acquainted and were advised as to needed equipment and supplies. Janet quickly became "just one of the guys," getting dirty, greasy, assembling and disassembling airplane engines. After classes we would gather together in a garage at 47th Street and Wabash Avenue to discuss difficult subject matter. It was at one such gathering that we organized the Challenger Air Pilots' Association. Johnny Robinson was elected as the association's first president. Janet became very interested in the club, and it was a huge success.

With this progression of activities came the need for our own aircraft. Fortunately, Robinson and Coffey were both already pilots. But it was Janet who bought the first licensed airplane, an OX-5 International. It is believed that this was possibly the first licensed airplane owned and operated by a colored female.

Funding aviation activities was difficult during the early 1930s. However, Janet always came up with fund-raising ideas such as quarter parties, dances, and so on. In fact there were difficulties every step of the way. Now that Janet had provided an airplane, where were we going to hangar it? Airfields refused to rent space to people of color. This, too, was overcome. A large field was located in Robbins, Illinois, a small black community south of Chicago, on which we built a hangar ourselves and cleared the grounds of trees, rocks, and other debris. Things went well until a windstorm destroyed the hangar and our two airplanes.

Later we moved to Harlem Airport in Oak Lawn, a Chicago suburb. Janet continued her flying activities and also began writing a column on aviation for the *Chicago Defender* newspaper. In 1946 she purchased another airplane, a Piper PA-12 Super Cruiser, in which she logged many hours of cross-country flying. Janet also made this plane available for others to fly at minimum cost.

Janet was indeed "just one of the guys," but one great guy!

C. Alfred "Chief" Anderson

Janet was the victim of prejudice which all pioneer black aviators had to overcome. I first met this dear lady when she flew her plane to Tuskegee to receive flight training to qualify for a commercial license. I myself was instructing on another flight program, and she was assigned to instructor Ray Thomas. She completed this commercial flight course with a satisfactory grade.

The next step was to receive a flight check from an FAA flight examiner in order to receive this license. This flight check was given by Inspector T. K. Hudson on his day at Tuskegee to give checks for various licenses. Upon completion of this flight check, she was told that she had satisfactorily passed all requirements for a commercial license, but that he knew of no other colored female with such a license and he was not going to be the first one to issue such a license.

But that didn't stop Janet. As she often said, "Every defeat was a challenge."

Cornelius R. Coffey

Janet Harmon Bragg was a good friend to me, to the late John C. Robinson, and to aviation in general. She was one of the most unselfish persons you could ever expect to meet. She practically supported the Challenger group single-handedly and never complained.

After Johnny Robinson and I graduated from the Curtiss Wright Flying Service master mechanics course, the doors were open to other black students. Johnny and I had opened the doors to an approved aviation school, and that door was to remain open forever to black students.

Janet was one of the first, along with some 30 to 35 other students, and one of the things that stumped me for some time was why she wanted to become an aircraft and engine mechanic. She was a registered nurse, and *employed,* and a godsend to the group. She invited us to her home and entertained the group many times. She was the first in the new group of students to purchase an airplane, and she gave permission for the group to use it. She owned several airplanes after that and still remained the unselfish person I had met many years before, willing to do her part for the cause of aviation.

I would like to relate a little incident involving our angel of mercy. We had completed a meeting of pilots visiting Chicago; several days after the meeting I had to go to Lock Haven, Pennsylvania, to pick up a new Piper Cub for our school program. While waiting for the weather to clear for my takeoff for home, I heard an aircraft over the airport flying in and out of the low clouds. I spotted a WACO F and thought, could this be B. J. Strode's aircraft? It sounded familiar. The pilot finally spotted the airport and landed. It was B. J. all right, and he had Janet in the front seat with her shoes off. She told me that if she had to die she wanted her shoes off. She explained that they had been lost and had been trying to read the names of the towns on the railroad signs on the depots, which is awfully dangerous in the Allegheny Mountains area. I told them I had received word every 15 minutes and had decided to wait out the weather, which I felt B. J. should have done. Janet told me of many close shaves they had had after refueling the aircraft. Nevertheless, Strode wanted to take off and continue his flight to New York. I tried to tell him to wait for the weather to clear a little more, but he took off anyway. A short time later he came back and landed. This time he almost cracked up the airplane!

Strode had been in such a hurry he had not even checked his aircraft after it was refueled. The line boy failed to lock the cap on his oil tank, and it came off and sprayed oil over the windshield. By the

time the ship was cleaned up the weather had cleared for our takeoff, theirs to New York and mine to Chicago.

Luckily, B. J. and Janet completed their trip to New York and returned to Chicago safely. B. J. returned to his home in Galveston, Texas. Later he purchased a twin-engine UC-78 Cessna and, on a trip from Texas to Florida, failed to heed another bad weather report and flew into a violent storm. He, his mother, and his pastor were lost, without a trace of the aircraft found for many years.

Getting back to Janet: God blessed her for her kind deeds and her helping hand to those in need. I am thinking of the many Ethiopian students she helped, and her resulting trips to Ethiopia. I came within six months of a trip to Ethiopia myself, but Italy invaded Ethiopia and the trip had to be canceled. I often think about how close I came to making that trip. But God had other plans for me. I have always tried to follow His advice, and I thank Him many times a day for allowing me to keep my hands in His hands. Wherever He leads me I will gladly follow.

In June 1979 a young Ethiopian contacted me for a mechanics examination. He wanted to take his FAA power plant and mechanics examination, and after his test we began to talk about his homeland. I told him about my planned trip in 1935 and why I wasn't able to go. He told me that his father had told him about an American who had to leave in 1936 but returned in 1944 and had an accident, died, and was buried in Addis Ababa, the capital. He was shocked to find out that the man was my dear friend John C. Robinson, one of the best friends I ever had or expected to know.

This young man told me that things were not the same in Ethiopia, and that most of the good people who had known the emperor, Haile Selassie, were trying to leave the country. He wanted to become an American citizen. He had worked for the Ethiopian airline as an apprentice mechanic, and I found him to be well trained. I tried to help him locate a permanent job with an airline.

Janet often mentioned her concern about the youth of America, and particularly the youth in our large cities and how they might be

helped. I have worked with young people for many years, and it really tears me up to see how today's youth are racing away without any hope of being useful to humanity. Who knows how many good leaders and professional people there could be with a helping hand? If something isn't done soon, we can count this an almost lost generation and a sad day indeed.

In 1943 I got permission from the parents of six of my civil pilot training club members to allow me to teach them to fly at the age of 15, and to solo them as a present for their 16th birthdays. At 17 years they could receive their private pilot's certificates. Each one of these students was a success. One of them was Earl Renfroe Jr. When I met his dad at the Tuskegee Airmen's meeting in Chicago in 1979, he told me that Earl Jr. was then a full colonel in the Air Force.

These are the things that bring tears of joy. They remind me of the help I was able to give students, if only a word of encouragement. They want to thank me for my efforts, and it is a good feeling to know that they have not forgotten. I will always be willing to work with any program that can help remedy our sad situation, and with God's help we will find a way. He will never fail to answer a prayer.

Certainly Janet Harmon Bragg never failed to help anyone who called on her for assistance.

Index

Accra, Ghana, 88
Acres Field, Chicago, 29
Addis Ababa, Ethiopa, 62, 64, 73,
   75, 77, 89, 91, 111
Adopt-a-School program, 103
Aeronautical University, xx, 26, 29.
   See also Curtiss Wright Flying
   Service
Africa Hall, Addis Ababa, 64
Aid to Dependent Children, 59
Allen, George, 48–49, 50
Anderson, Charles Alfred "Chief,"
   39, 41, 43–44, 48, 51–52, 94,
   96, 98, 101, 102, 109

Anderson, "Dynamite," 29
Anderson, Gertrude, 52, 101
Andrew Hospital, 21
Arizona, University of, 104
Armstrong, Neil, 98
Army Nurse Corps, xxi
Arrington, Mike, 90
Arrington's Travel Agency, 90
Art Institute of Chicago, 64, 65
Asmara, Ethiopa, 91
Assayus, Nerayo, 62, 63–64, 73–74,
   76
Athens, Greece, 71–72
Atlanta, Ga., 33–34

Austria, 92
Axum, Ethiopia, 91
Azene, Muleneh, 65, 83

Barat College of the Sacred Heart, 83
Batts, Grandmother, 5
Batts, Oss (grandfather), 1–2, 4, 5
Batts, Pete, 54
Batts, Sally, 54
Beeks, Cordia (niece), 22
Beeks, Janie, 8
Bethune, Mary McLeod, 38
Betsch, John Thomas, Sr., xiii
Bishop Wright Air Industry Award, 97–98
Black Heritage Week, 95
Black History Month, 94, 96
"Black Wings" exhibition at the National Air and Space Museum, xiv, xvi, 95–96
Black Women in Science, ix
Bloomington, Ill., 61–62, 63
Blue Island, Ill., xxi
Blue Nile, 77
"Blue Vein Society," 10
Bluford, Guion S., Jr., 95
Blumeris, Arthur, 89, 104
Blumeris, Iris, xv
Blumeris, Michael, xv, 89, 104
Blumeris, Tseganet, xv, 81, 89, 104
Boaz, Ala., 45, 48
Bohr, Paul K., 96
Bowens, Johnny, 103
Bragg, Janet Harmon: accomplishments of, xi–xii; and the Adopt-a-School program, 103; birth of, 1, 2; childhood of, xx, 2–12; and Civilian Pilot Training Program

(CPTP), 24–41; death of, ix, xxi; death of father, 22; death of husband, Sumner, 104; death of mother, 55; discrimination against, 34, 40–41, 51–52, 53; divorce of, 21–22; earning of commercial pilot's certificate by, xxi, 50; education of, 3, 9–10; employment at Metropolitan Burial Insurance Association, 23–24, 26, 44, 53, 55; employment at Palmer House, 19–20; employment at Wilson Hospital, 20–21; first cross-country flight of, 31; first visit to Ethiopia, 69–79; flight to attend Graduate Nurses Association meeting, 33–34; flight training of, xix–xx, 26–29; and foreign students, 61–68, 81–92; friends' and colleagues' memories of, 107–12; friendship with Haile Selassie, 25; heart attack of, 102; honors for, 93–98; interest in flying, 25; learning to drive, 6; licensing of, 30n; marriage to Evans Waterford, 21–22; marriage to Sumner Bragg, 55; move to North, 15–24; move to Tucson, 104; name of, 3; as nurse, xx–xxi, 15–16, 18–24; nurse's training of, 12–13; receipt of Outstanding Citizen of Tucson award, 103; rejection of, for WASPs, 40–41; religious life of, 8–9; retirement of, from nursing home business, 59–60; seeking of city public health job, 22–23; taking of licensing exam by, 18, 31–32;

and turning of Wanzer mansion into Harmon-Bragg nursing home, 55–60; at Tuskegee Institute, 43–52; and U.S. visit of Haile Selassie, 66–68
Bragg, Sumner (husband), xii, xvi, 55, 57, 60, 67, 69, 78, 79, 86, 90, 92, 103, 104
"Bronzeville" (Chicago's South Side), 17
Brooks, John, 8–9
Brown, Edgar G., 38
Brown, Willa, 28, 36, 39, 99
Buhl Pup, 32, 33
Bullard, Eugene, 26
Burroughs, Ken, 27

Cairo, Egypt, 89–90
Campbell, Clifford, 65–66, 81
Capital Dairy, 57
Carey, Willie, 17
Carver, George Washington, laboratory, 48
Catholic Charities, 54
Cessna 172, 30
Challenger Aero Club, 29
Challenger Air Pilots' Association, 32, 35, 108
Chanute, Octave, 60
Chanute Field, 53
Chicago, University of, 84; lab school at, 81
Chicago Air Route Traffic Control Center, 93
Chicago Defender newspaper, 26, 36, 108
Chicago Graduate Nurses Association, 19, 23, 86
Chicago Medical School, 21

Chicago Metropolitan Assurance Company, 23
Chicago Midway Airport, 67
Chicago Municipal Airport, 52
Churback, L. M., 27
Civil Aeronautics Authority (CAA), 38–39
Civilian Pilot Training Program (CPTP), 28, 32, 33, 35–41
Cochran, Jacqueline, 40
Coffey, Cornelius, xx, 27–33, 36, 37, 61, 96, 98, 107, 108, 109–12
Coffey School of Aeronautics, at Harlem Airport, 39
Coffey's Civil Air Patrol (CAP) squadron, 28
Cole, Johnnetta B., 102
Cole, Robert, 44, 45
Coleman, Bessie, xiii, xix, 26, 44, 99, 108
Columbus, Ga., 50
Commandaire biplane, 32
Cook County Hospital, 18, 22, 54, 59; School of Nursing at, 22
Copenhagen, 92
Cosby, Albert, 30
Cosby, Bill, 102–3
Cosby, Camille, 102
CPTP. *See* Civilian Pilot Training Program (CPTP)
Cumberland River, 45
Curtiss Wright Flying Service, 26, 27, 109. *See also* Aeronautical University

Dakar, Senegal, 84
Davis, Benjamin O., Jr., 94
Davis, Frances Lucille, 13
Davis, Fred, 16–17

Davis, Queenie, 37
Davis-Monthan Air Force Base, 96
Debebe, Mulatu, 65–66, 76–78
Decatur, Ala., 32
Denmark, 92
DePriest, Bertha, 17
Devit, David, 88–89
Dick, Maurice, 57
Dickens, Janie, 3
Dirksen, Everett McKinley, 38
Dorothy Hall, Tuskegee Institute, 47, 48
Dunbar Vocational School, 65

Ebenezer Baptist Church, 58
Engen, Donald, 96
Eritrea, 91
Ethiopia, 32–33, 61, 64, 66
Ethiopian Airlines, 71, 75, 91
Ethiopian Coptic Christian Church, 76
Ethiopian Herald, 76
Ex-Chicagoans, 103
Experimental Aircraft Association Air Adventure Museum, 95–96

FAA World, xiv
Falashas, 91
Federal Aviation Administration (FAA) Great Lakes region, xiii, xiv
Fédération Aéronautique Internationale (FAI) pilot's license, 99
Finland, 92
Fisk University, 45, 55
Ford, Charles "Chuck," 98, 103
Ford, Doris, 98
Forney, Claudius, 22

Forsythe, Albert E., 43
Frankfurt, Germany, 65
Franklin Institute, 95
Freetown, Sierra Leone, 84
Frehewhoit, Lemme, 70
French Flying Service, 26

Galveston, Tex., 111
Garcia, Mrs., 19
Germany, 92
Giddings, Ann, 23
Glasco, Mattie, 10
Goldwater, Barry, 98
Gondar, Ethiopia, 91
Graduate Nurses Association, 33, 60; Chicago chapter of, 19, 23, 86
Gray, Jimmy, 12
Great Depression, 44
Green, Dwight H., 38, 63–64
Greene, Lillian, 10
Griffin, Ga., xx, xxi, 1, 12, 15, 25, 52

Haile, Zewditu, 65, 82–83
Hall, Pauline Dickens, 12
Hampton, Clyde, 95
Hardesty, Von, xiv, 94–95, 96
Harlem Airport (Oak Lawn, Ill.), 32, 33, 34, 37, 44, 45, 61, 94, 108
Harmon, Cordia Batts (mother), 1, 2–3, 6–7, 9, 34, 40–41, 54, 55
Harmon, Elza (sister), 2
Harmon, Evelyn (niece), 22
Harmon, Lillian (sister), 2
Harmon, Pat (brother), 2, 4, 10, 11, 26, 53–54, 62, 68
Harmon, Peter J. (brother), 2

Harmon, Samuel (brother), 2
Harmon, Samuel (father), 1, 2, 3, 8
Harmon, Viola "Honey" (sister), 2,
  7–8, 16, 48
Harmon-Bragg Nursing Home,
  55–60
Harra, Ethiopa, 75
Henderson, Ed, 15–16
Herbert, Maurice, 82
Herbert, Rachel, 82
Hopkins, Ellen Moore, 86–87
Hopkins, Richard, 86–87
Horne, Lena, 10
Howard University, 94, 103;
  FAA/NASA symposium at, xiv
Hudson, T. K., 50–51, 53, 109
Hudson Super 6, 11
Hunt, Harold, 10
Hunt, Rufus, 93–94
Huntsville, Ala., 45
Hurd, Harold, 31, 33, 36, 53, 95,
  96, 107–9

Illinois, University of, 63
Illinois College of Pharmacy, 82
Illinois Wesleyan University, 61–62

Jackson, Lewis, 98
Jackson, Manuella, 45, 46, 47, 48
Jackson, William, 107–8
James, Daniel "Chappie," Jr., 98,
  102
Jerusalem, 73
Johnson, Charles, 36, 39, 44–45,
  53
Johnson, Edward, 36
Johnson, Jackie, 52
Johnson, VeNona Roberts, xiv, 55,
  84–85, 89–90

Jones, Ed, 37
Jones, George, 37
Jones, Lola, 28

Kabbah, Patricia Tucker, 84–85
Kabbah, Tejan, 85
Kakata, Liberia, 86, 87
Kassa, Mr., 67, 68
Kelly, Edward J., 38
Kennedy International Airport, 49,
  97
Kennedy-King Junior College, 83
Kennelly, Martin, 67
Kibrat, Mimi, 92
Kibrat, Tedelee, 92
King, Beatrice, 92
Koldheimen, Anna, 89
Kriz, Marjorie, xiii–xiv

LaGuardia Field, 49
Lake Tana, 77
La Toure, Art, 37
LeMoyne-Owen College, 21
Lewing, Fred, 44
Liberia, 49, 85–86
Links Cotillion, 82
Lock Haven, Pa., 110
London, 71
Lopez, Donald, 94
Louis, Joe, 21
Luce, Clare Boothe, 47n
Luce, Henry, 47n

Mack, Emil, 27
MacVicar Hospital, 12–13, 15, 21
Makonnen, Endalkatchew, 67–68,
  75
Makonnen, Tseganet, 78
Malone, Anne, 33

Marian, Haile, 87–88
Marian, Minetta, 54
Masai Mara, 91
Matlock, Frances, xiv, 55
Meharry Medical College School of
    Nursing, 23
Meskal Day, 72–73, 91
Meskal Square, 73
Metropolitan Burial Insurance
    Association, 23–24, 44, 53, 56
Mexico, 92
Midway Airport, 52
Mobile, Ala., 13
Monrovia, Liberia, 86
Moore, Frances Scott, xiv–xv, xxi,
    12, 54, 56
Moton Field, Tuskegee Institute, 46
Murphy, Doris, 28
Murray, Walter, 33
Museum of Science and Industry,
    60, 95

Nairobi, Kenya, 91
Nash, Grover, xv, 31, 32, 33, 36,
    53
Nashville, Tenn., 45
National Aeronautics and Space
    Administration, 13
National Air and Space Museum
    (NASM), xii, xiii, xiv, 94, 98;
    "Black Wings" exhibition at xiv,
    xvi, 95–96
National Airmen's Association of
    America (NAAA), 36–37, 39, 96
National Trust for Historic
    Preservation, 101–2
National Youth Administration, 38
Negro Airmen International, 94, 101
Negro History Week, 94

Nelms, Cora, 11
Nimmons, Cora Lee, 3
Northwestern University, 57, 63,
    83
Norway, 92

Old Pueblo International
    Communications Club, 96
Onassis, Jacqueline, 105
Outstanding Citizen of Tucson
    award, 103
Owens, Ky., 33
Ox-5 International, 30, 108

Palmer House, 20
Pal-Waukee Airport, 31–32, 52
Pan American Goodwill Flight, 43
Paris, 71
Parrish, Mrs. Noel, xvi
Parrish, Noel, 51
Phillips, Biddy, 11–12
Pima Air and Space Museum, 101
Pima Community College, 104
Piper Cherokee 140, 30
Piper Cruiser, 39, 108–9
Piper Cub, 33, 39, 66, 110
Piper PA-12 Super Cruiser, 108–9
Pisano, Dominick, xiv, 95, 96
Policy rackets, 37n
Powell, William J., 30n
Protestant Ecumenical Council, 98
Provident Hospital, Chicago, 18;
    School of Nursing at, 17

Queen Mary, 69–70, 71

Ras Hotel, Addis Ababa, 73
Renfroe, Earl, Jr., 112
Rich, Doris L., xiii

Ritter, Mr., 52
Robbins Air Field, 108
Robinson, Bill "Bojangles," 19
Robinson, John, xx, 27–33, 61–62, 75, 107, 108, 109, 111
Robinson, Theodore W., 98
Robinson, Walter, 44–46
Rockford, Ill., 16
Rome, 72, 90, 92
Roosevelt, Eleanor, 38, 39
Roosevelt, Franklin D., 38
Roosevelt University, 64

St. Clair, Marie, 28, 36
St. Stephens, 9; Episcopal school at, 9
Sampson, Daisy, 23
Sarah Lawrence College, 86
Scott, E. Jewell, 52
Scott, Frances, 12
Selam, Alle Felege, 64, 73–74, 76
Selam, Teodros, 65
Selassie, Haile, xv, xxi, 25, 32, 61, 64, 66–68, 69, 71, 73–75, 79, 103–4, 111
Selassie, Haile, International Airport, 73
Selassie, Haregone, 81
Selassie, Seifu, 78, 81
Selleke, Seifu, 62, 63, 88, 104–5
Selma, Ala., 49
Sheehy, Ethel, 40
Sherwood, Ohio, 37
Sierra Leone, 84–85
Simonson, Joseph, 76–77
Singapore, 92
Smith, Ida Van, 97
Smith, Ida Van, Flight Club, 97
Smith, James, 46

Smith, Lillian, 71
Smith, Roland, 16
Smith, Viola, 16–17
Smithsonian World, 96
Sneed, Edward (Mike), 22–23
Southern Illinois University, 82
Spelman Seminary (later College), viii–ix, xx, 12–13, 15, 102
Spencer, Chauncey, 36, 37, 39
Springfield, Ill., 18
Stockholm, 92
Stokes, Margaret, 11
Strickland, Patricia, 39n
Strode, B. J., 110–11
Sudan, 72
Sweden, 92

Talbot, David, 75–76
Taylor, Elizabeth, 105
Teshome, Zennebework, 82
Texas Tech University, 65
Theophilus, Abuna, 76, 77
Thomas, Ray, 49, 109
Thompson, Charles, 86
Thompson, Frankie, 86
Thompson, William, 95
Travel Air, 29
Trophy, Thompson, 31
Truman, Harry S, 38, 39
Tucson, 60
Tulane University, 63
Turner, Roscoe, 31
Tuskegee Army Air Field, 46
Tuskegee Institute, 3, 12, 16, 32, 39, 41, 43–52
Tuskegee University, 101

UC-78 Cessna, 111
Uniontown, Ala., 49

United Negro College Fund, 102
U.S. Army Air Corps, 38

Wabash Avenue YMCA, 36
Wanzer, Sidney, 55
Washington, Booker T., monument, 48
Waterford, Evans (first husband), 21–22
Waters, Enoch P., Jr., 36
Watkins, Leon, 96–97
Weaver, Dorothy, 28
Wells, Dorothy, 33
Wells, William, 33
White, Dale, 36, 37, 39

Williams, George, 36
Wilson Hospital, 18, 21
Women's Auxiliary Service Pilots (WASP), xxi, 40–41
Woodson, Carter G., Library, 94
Works Progress Administration (WPA), 37
World Council of Churches, 63
World Health Organization, 63, 88
Wossen, Asfa, 75

Young, John, III, 49
Young, Perry, 49

Zimmerman, Mr., 33